Endorsements

"As a parent, Gaye James shares her journey with the reader as a mother of a child with selective mutism. *Living Beyond the Silence* allows the reader to gain insight into the daily lives of such children, the developmental course of the condition, and the experiences of caregivers devoted to helping them overcome this often misunderstood anxiety disorder."

—Angela E. McHolm, Ph.D., Helping Your Child with Selective Mutism: Practical Steps to Overcome a Fear of Speaking

"Selective mutism is a relatively rare anxiety disorder typically found in young children. If left untreated, the mute behavior can be unintentionally reinforced and thus increasingly difficult to treat. Gaye James, the author of *Living Beyond the Silence,* shares her story to raise awareness of this disorder."

—Myra Cotton-Thomas, Ed.S., NCSP,
Public School Psychologist

"*Living Beyond the Silence* gives a unique perspective of selective mutism from a parent's viewpoint. Gaye takes you on the journey through the disorder as she shares her experiences raising a child with selective mutism. A mother's perspective is so imperative to helping others. I have had the personal advantage of knowing both Gaye and her son, Trevor. And I am thrilled to be a part of this new adventure."

—Heather L Hensley, M.S., CCC, SLP
(Speech Language Pathologist)

In *Living Beyond the Silence*, Gaye James seeks to raise awareness of selective mutism. By sharing her own beautifully written and engaging story, her book will undoubtedly provide much needed understanding and encouragement to families seeking help for a child struggling in silence.

—Sue Bingham Herring, Licensed Mental Health Counselor,
Board-Certified Expert in Traumatic Stress,
author of The Scent of Safety – A Novel

"By sharing her struggles raising a child with selective mutism, Gaye James is helping bring awareness to the debilitating disorder. Her parental viewpoint offers an inside look at the anxiety and gives hope to others."

—Carol Weinert, LPCC
(Licensed Professional Clinical Counselor)

"In *Living Beyond the Silence*, Gaye James does an outstanding job of spreading awareness about selective mutism. As a veteran teacher, I have worked with several students who have selective mutism. Gaye's book is an excellent resource for both parents and teachers alike. I highly recommend this enlightening, compassionate book."

—Staci Montgomery, teacher, Harold Schnell Elementary

"Young children need advocates, especially when they struggle with misunderstood issues. Gaye James is advocating for those struggling with selective mutism by writing her book, *Living Beyond the Silence*. Using her own experience as an example, she is educating the public and bringing awareness to the disorder."

—Tanya Rowe, B.S., Human Services Management

Living Beyond the Silence

Living Beyond the Silence

Learning to Overcome Selective Mutism, Severe Shyness, and Other Childhood Anxieties

GAYE JAMES

Printed in the United States of America

Published by Author Academy Elite
P.O. Box 43, Powell, OH 43035
www.AuthorAcademyElite.com

Paperback ISBN –978-1-64746-513-1
Hardcover ISBN-978-1-64746-514-8
Ebook ISBN-978-1-64746-515-5
Library of Congress Control Number: 2020918140

For Trevor Cox

Thank you for your inspiration.
Without you, my son, there would be no story to share.

Contents

Part 3:
Winning The War On Selective Mutism

Appendices

Note to the Reader

Whatever guided you to this point in your life and drove you to this book, I am pleased you have joined me on my journey through selective mutism. Maybe you have heard of this anxiety disorder and are passionate to learn more. Maybe this is an entirely new concept to you, and you're eager to open your mind, willing to understand this foreign disorder. Or maybe you have a shy child you're concerned about helping. Whatever brought you here, I appreciate your investment in this book of hope.

My name is Gaye (not Gayle, Gail, or Gayla). You may be able to relate to the endless butchering of names, especially today when unique names are prevalent. Do I like my name? Well, that's an entirely different subject. But it was the name given to me upon my birth, so I embrace it. Sometimes life gives us struggles we would never choose to endure. But I believe there is a reason for everything we encounter. And often after overcoming an obstacle, we find we are stronger and ready to take on the next. If we let fear guide us, we'll never truly live freely. Fear scares away happiness.

I wrote this book to help others who may be struggling silently. By telling my story of raising a child with selective mutism and learning to live beyond the silence, I offer hope to others. And my son is proof you can overcome selective mutism, severe shyness, or other anxiety disorders you may be facing.

Everything I have written in this book is true to the best of my knowledge and memory. Conversations are as I recall them. Our journey through this painful voice-paralyzing disorder was a difficult path, but there is life on the other side. All suggestions for treatment options and helpful hints are merely that: suggestions. They are not intended to take the place of professional medical assistance, only to offer further understanding of this disorder. The more you know about the illness, the better equipped you are to teach your child how to overcome their challenges.

Welcome to the beginning of your journey through the darkness. See you on the other side. And remember, you are not alone.

—Gaye

Meeting Selective Mutism

The sun shone down, reflecting off the pavement and lighting up the sidewalk leading to the preschool building. All the parents were proudly marching their children toward the school for the first day. Some of the kids' excitement converted into energy. They jumped off the brick wall surrounding the flower garden or the large rock near the path heading back to St. James Preschool, which was hidden behind the church. The air buzzed with heightened emotion, and smiles were shared by everyone around. It was day one of their new life, and all the children embraced the upcoming adventure.

I glanced down at my own four-year-old son's precious face. He was wide-eyed and interested. Today was the beginning of something new and mysterious. We shared a smile over the unknown possibilities this moment held. Trevor had been looking forward to this the whole summer. Ever since we signed him up, preschool had been his main topic of conversation. He would often tell his big brother, Josh, all about what he was going to accomplish when he began. Josh would share stories about his preschool days some four years earlier while his little brother soaked it in like a sponge. I imagine Trevor wanted to reenact many of Josh's tales, hoping his experience would live up to the same level of hype. Although, after our private tour a few weeks prior, Trevor's focus was the treehouse room. He couldn't wait to climb up the ladder and slide down the slides. To be honest, that room spoke to me, too, calling me to join in on the fun. I mean, who wouldn't want to climb a tree that filled an entire room with slides emptying into the center onto colorful, padded floor mats?

A witch approached, startling us out of our imaginations. Mrs. Gronefeld had been the lead preschool teacher for more years than Trevor had been alive, possibly even longer than I had been alive. The wiry, jet black-haired woman smiled warmly, and her deep eyes held a story of wisdom and experience. Her witch's hat caught the attention of all the nearby children, which was apparently her intent. They were drawn to her, intoxicated by her eccentricities. Trevor gazed upon the scene, engrossed in the interaction between the other children and his new teacher. She spoke briefly to each family, trying to spread love and reassurance while introducing herself to each member of the new class.

Mrs. Gronefeld smiled in our direction as she made her way toward us through the swarm of people. She nodded at me, then turned her full attention to Trevor, "Hi, I am Mrs. Gronefeld. I'm your new teacher this year. What is your name, young man?"

Knowing my son's high level of excitement about today, I expected to hear him answer with an enthusiastic "Trevor." Instead, his little arms clung tightly to my leg as his face paled and eyes widened. He stood there frozen like a deer in the headlights of a car, unable to move. The smile on Mrs. Gronefeld's face wavered for a moment, but she promptly regained her composure.

After a glance down at her roster, she deduced which child was standing in her presence and said, "I believe you are Trevor. Is that correct?" Pausing a moment in anticipation of his answer, her query was met with silence from my petrified child. He gave no response, not even a nod in confirmation from the tiny body still attached to my leg.

"Yes, this is Trevor," I answered. "He's a little shy today, overwhelmed by all the excitement, I think." The excuse flowed smoothly from my lips as my motherly protection mode kicked in. But he wasn't shy—not my son. He seemed to love attention at home.

Looking back on that moment, I now know why he responded so dramatically. Trevor has selective mutism. But at that time in 2001, I was dumbfounded by his reaction. I suppose starting from the beginning would be the best approach to explaining our journey through this speech-paralyzing anxiety and how we helped our child learn to use his voice again.

PART 1

Breaking the Lie: "He's Just Shy"

CHAPTER 1

Beating the Bullies

Elementary school is challenging for many children, but those of us who are different struggle the most. I still remember the first day I became a target of teasing. It was the early 1970s, and my family had moved three times that year. To add to my frustration over having to start again in another new school, an older boy overheard my name and immediately yelled, "Gaye is gaaaay!" My confused reaction did not satisfy his quest for dominance, so he decided to explain to me why it was so hilarious. "Don't you know what gays are? Faggots, that's what, and you're one of 'em. You like girls and are gonna marry one someday."

Even though I was still clueless as to why I should be upset, I knew his snarky words were said in hatred, and they stabbed through me like a sharp blade. Tears of embarrassment spontaneously trickled down my cheeks. The last thing I wanted to be at that impressionable age was different, and this boy pointed out to all within earshot that I was indeed different.

Years of tears passed before I felt confident to face the name-shaming bullies. Changing my name twice in elementary school was one of my coping methods, but at the ripe old age of twelve, I finally felt emotionally mature enough to handle being called gay. Maybe entering middle school gave me a false strength or the realization that no matter what I do in life, someone will try to knock me down, so I might as well embrace my differences. Whatever the reasoning, I did it. I became . . . Gaye. By that time in my life, I had heard all the jokes one could muster regarding my name, so often I'd beat a new acquaintance to the punch with my own teasing. "Hi, my name is Gaye, but I'm not gay in case you were wondering."

I recall once meeting a friend of a friend, who was a snobby, cold-hearted, spiteful teenage girl. Even her handshake gave off a flair of pretentiousness, only brushing my fingers briefly with hers as if she would contract a lower-class status if our palms made contact. When my friend introduced me, the princess immediately threw out the most common reaction from immature personalities upon hearing my name for the first time.

"Are you gay?" she asked, flipping her hair from one side to the other as all proper princesses should do when meeting the lower class.

I squeezed her fingers tightly and pulled her toward me, then whispered into her ear, "We can talk about that later." I gave her a little wink, and she quickly pulled her hand back. Her appalled expression fed my strength and determination, although we never did talk about that later.

I believe the pain and suffering in our lives is meant to strengthen and prepare us for what is to come. My childhood of being teased about my name taught me how to persevere through challenges, often anticipating pain and preventing the torture. Understanding the deep hurt bullying can generate helped prepare me for dealing with anxiety issues and taught me patience. Little did I realize at the time it was preparing me to help my own child.

Fast-forward to adulthood when my life altered from its singular direction. I met my first husband when I was eighteen. He was quirky and funny, and he always made me laugh. Upon learning his surname was Cox, I imagined how my new name would be perceived by the world if we were to marry. The words "Gaye Cox" had an alternative meaning. I had two choices: not to pursue a relationship with this man and prevent any ridicule I might encounter or stand strong against the bullies and accept the awkwardness. Maybe the rebelliousness in me urged me to continue forward and embrace the new quest. Because I chose to stand firm and take on this new identity. I became Gaye Cox and dared anyone to scoff at me.

My new father-in-law was a taciturn man. I believe wholeheartedly he had the selective mutism gene that was passed on to our son. But during his life there was no commonly known designation for his profound anxiety other than shyness. A friend of the family admitted to me once, "If he's said five words in the ten years I've known him, I'd be surprised," which validated my suspicions.

Knowing where it came from didn't lessen the stress of the disorder, and had I known there was a risk of having a child with this anxiety, my path would not have changed. I could have been alerted to the onset of signs much sooner, however, potentially helping my son deal with this burden before it took full control of his life and ours.

While the obvious lack of speaking is the primary symptom one associates with selective mutism, it is not the only struggle experienced. Looking back at those days with my father-in-law and his relationship with his family, there were clues to this mysterious disorder that had been disregarded. His whole personality was affected, creating an invisible barrier between him and his children. The crippling anxiety dominated every aspect of his life, preventing his emotions from surfacing. He found it easier to talk to a stranger than to his own children. Not that talking to a stranger was a simple task for him either. Still, the established family relationship rules had already been set years prior in his mind.

An opportunity was presented to me to say a few words at my former father-in-law's funeral nearly two decades after meeting him. Writing his eulogy was challenging, to say the least, but I finally decided on creating a poem. How does one use words to describe someone who doesn't use words? Here was my reflection.

A Father, a husband, a grandfather, an uncle, a brother, a friend -
Whatever title you used to describe him, he was still Jerry Lee Cox.

This was a man who enjoyed taking in his world while standing in the shadows.

You would often see him smiling quietly as the crowd spoke on, enjoying every moment of his visitors in a way only he knew.

Jerry had a hidden sense of humor, often a practical joker.
Those who were close to him were fortunate to experience the many facets of his personality.

He loved his family, though he often found it difficult to express his feelings in words. His eyes would sparkle with emotion whenever his grandchildren were near.

Jerry was a proud man, an honorable man.
He was driven by his strength, passion for life, and especially his belief in luck.

This man who many saw as a "man of few words" made his mark on this Earth.
With the help of his incredible wife, Joanne, he raised three children into strong, self-reliant adults.

This father, husband, grandfather, uncle, brother, and friend will be greatly missed, though he will remain in our hearts for always.

CHAPTER 2

Bonding Over Farting: New Beginnings

Becoming a mother was the first day I began to live. Life had a newfound focus and purpose. My firstborn son, Joshua, was a happy child. He was eager to learn and most content when being held. Nearly four years later his brother entered the scene. To say the two boys were as different as night and day might be extreme, but their personalities were unique from each other. Trevor, the youngest, was full of energy and particularly determined. Being held in our arms was only a mode for obtaining out-of-reach objects. Imagine trying to grasp a squirming piglet covered in mud. That was Trevor whenever anyone held him. He always had another agenda, his plan for when and how the world should react. If this perceived plan did not play out as expected, he would become upset and throw a tantrum. The terrible two's hit our home when he was one. Life was interesting, to say the least.

On his first birthday I sent out one-year announcements to the extended family with an adorable photo of Trevor sliding down the stairs (one of his favorite activities). Included on the announcement were a few words summarizing Trevor:

Wow, time flies when you're having fun, and our baby is turning ONE! Trevor is a healthy, happy toddler now. His favorite game is playing "pull the hair on the doggy" (or his brother—whomever he can grab faster). He runs everywhere and gets into everything . . . Life is fun!

Looking back, I would never have anticipated such a vocal, rambunctious child turning silent. But selective mutism does not happen instantly. It takes a multitude of factors to occur simultaneously before a child is plunged into muteness. A predisposition for anxiety is the strongest underlying component. Without this predisposition SM would not occur. It is an anxiety disorder. And even with this predisposition, most children under five are unlikely to suffer from it. It is uncommon, almost as unlikely as winning the lottery (which makes me wonder why we never played the lottery since obviously "luck" was on our side). Despite this, over the years experts are finding selective mutism is not as rare as originally thought, possibly because early on it might be misdiagnosed as autism or a developmental disorder. Many parents misunderstand the disorder and merely believe their child to be overly shy or defiant. They expect the child will "grow out of it" in time, and they may never seek professional help because of this misconception. I am confident this is how my ex-father-in-law's parents felt with their son.

Even though Trevor was energetic and excitable, he seemed like a normal toddler. Whenever we were around an actual hyperactive child, my appreciation of Trevor grew tenfold. He had his quirks, but he was never more than I could handle.

Like many other marriages, ours dissolved three years into Trevor's life. As a single mom I worked hard to maintain the boys' routines. Knowing how valuable a father-son relationship can be, I requested shared parenting. This nearly broke my heart. Not having my sons with me, especially to tuck in at night, was one of the most emotionally challenging situations I've endured. But I still believe it was the best choice for the children. They got to keep their parents and their life as they knew it. Allowing our family dog to stay with the house and big yard was another difficult decision. But it didn't seem fair to tote her along into the cramped apartment lifestyle.

The three-year-old toddler adjusted easily to a split family. The biggest obstacle was having to lug his prized personal belongings from house to house. So, we began using a black bag to transport the items. Anything important went into the black bag, and Trevor learned this pattern quickly. He thrived on routines and order. There were still incidences of forgotten rag ball pants or cleats, but overall our system played out flawlessly.

Even though money was an issue in my single-parent life, I felt spending time together was invaluable. So, we took a brief trip, only the three of us (Josh, Trevor, and me) during Josh's spring break. Little did I know at the time this trip would be the first of a strong annual tradition in our family, continuing until adulthood. Our first "spring break" wasn't glamorous and didn't include any beach scenes as many do during this time of year. Our budget took us across the state border to a hotel with a spinning restaurant at the top and a small community park below. Those few days of together time were greatly needed and helped strengthen our family bond. Taking a break from the everyday stresses is important, especially when dealing with a child with an anxiety disorder.

Nick entered our lives when Trevor was three and a half years of age. We dated an entire summer before he met the children. My hesitancy was to ensure a stable relationship was maintained before their introduction. Knowing Trevor's tendency toward routines and rules, I didn't want to create any unnecessary disruption in his life. Once I knew our relationship was strong and stable, I introduced him to the boys. Nick visited us one evening, and he met Josh first. Reaching forward with a handshake gesture toward the nearly-seven-year-old melted my heart. Seeing this grown man treat my child with such respect immediately won me over. Trevor's meeting played out a little differently, but he was only half Josh's age. Upon me calling for the three-year-old to come out of his room to meet Nick, Trevor responded by running full speed toward the big man sitting on the couch. He dove onto his lap with such force that gas expelled (quite loudly) upon his landing. Nick laughed, exclaiming, "That's my boy!" Trevor seemed pleased by this man's response at his playful entrance. He may not remember the moment today as an adult, but the emotional connection created by that single incident would last a lifetime. Only men can bond over farting.

CHAPTER 3

Beyond Shyness

The first sign that Trevor was not like other children became apparent only after being around strangers in public. At home Trevor was as loud as any other three-year-old struggling to find his inside voice. When outside of the home, he was a typical noisy toddler. It wasn't until a stranger spoke to him directly that his demeanor changed. But this is common, right? Other children suddenly get quiet and better behaved when a stranger enters the scene. It did not seem odd—at first.

My sister, Sharon, was Trevor's first babysitter while I worked part-time away from home. She watched him until he was about three and a half years of age, but she didn't notice anything unusual about Trevor's behavior, even though they never conversed. Having an older sibling made Trevor's life much easier as Josh would often interpret for him. No attention was drawn to the fact that he wasn't using his own voice, and Trevor was quite skilled at the gesture of pointing to obtain his heart's desires.

Jean was Trevor's first babysitter outside of the family, an elderly woman with a brusque personality. Several children were enrolled in her private daycare-like home. Initially, knowing his tendency toward routines and structure, I thought Trevor would thrive in this setting.

But he did not appear to enjoy it at Jean's. He would tell me, "It's ok," when asked to describe his day, often acting out with tantrums as soon as we returned home. Upon questioning Jean about Trevor's interactions and daily routine, she would list how long he had free play, what he ate for lunch, and what toys were his focus. Jean was pleased he was not a noisy child, often voicing her appreciation of this characteristic. At the time Trevor was resistive to sitting on the potty, so we allowed him to wear disposable pull-up training pants. We assumed he would potty train when he was ready and didn't wish to force him into it before he felt comfortable. He had not managed his own hygiene up to this point, so changing his pull-up was part of his regular care. Jean knew this when we first hired her, assuring me it wouldn't be a problem while she passive-aggressively bragged about potty training her granddaughter at eighteen months of age. Looking back, I believe Jean thought she could fix Trevor. Instead, I think she broke him more.

One afternoon as I arrived to pick up Trevor, Jean was changing his pull-up. She seemed rushed and admitted to running a little behind her typical schedule. Glancing down at my son's face, I discovered tears streaming down his cheeks. Immediately I asked him what happened, but he only stood there crying silently. Jean acted as if nothing was wrong, stating she hadn't noticed anything unusual. I paid her for her services, and off we went. At home in our familiar environment, Trevor began to feel comfortable enough to admit the reason for his tears. He explained, "Jean called me a baby and said I was too big for diapers." His tears returned as he recalled the harsh words that stung his pride. We knew most children were already potty trained at this age, but Trevor was his own person and should have been allowed to progress at his own pace. Anger soared through my veins as I listened to my precious little boy's disheartening recount of the event. A scar had formed on his self-image, etching a lasting impression into his mind.

Unsure if Trevor could overhear my phone conversation with Jean that evening, I attempted to control my animosity and refrained from cussing. It was difficult to get my point across without the use of such strong and powerful four-letter words. I managed to fire her, but I feared the damage to my child remained. Maybe there are worse derogatory terms, but being called a baby by a trusted adult was traumatizing for our young son. This became a pivotal moment in Trevor's life.

Experts previously believed selective mutism is brought on by a traumatic event. But more recently they are identifying PTSD (post-traumatic stress disorder) and traumatic mutism separately from SM. Trauma can activate SM in a predisposed child, but traumatic mutism exhibits differently. In a child with traumatic mutism, they are suddenly silent in all situations of life after the trauma occurs. For example, a child who witnesses the death of a parent or other situations evoking strong emotional reactions they are unable to process may experience sudden muteness. They become unable to speak to anyone, including loved ones, and have great difficulty dealing with reenactments of the traumatic incident. Selective mutism, on the other hand, typically exhibits as silence in public, but the child is still verbal at home. Social anxiety is SM's best friend. The two anxieties thrive off one another, enhancing the symptoms.

While Trevor's experience was traumatic for him at the time, he was able to process it with the support of his parents and family. I feel he did not immediately turn mute by shutting down from this incident. Working hard to be supportive of my child, I explained to Trevor the ugliness of life. Some people are naturally insensitive. Knowing he did not have to return to that environment again with the gruff babysitter helped Trevor immensely. But was it the underlying reason his selective mutism was triggered? We may never know.

The new babysitter, Julie, was a sweet and compassionate stay-at-home mother of two. She embraced the opportunity to watch Trevor. Her elementary-school-age children were only home during the summers when school was out of session, so their interactions were limited, but with their age differences it was probably for the best. During a typical day at Julie's, Trevor had the companionship of Samantha, my best friend's two-year-old daughter. Samantha's infant twin brothers monopolized Julie's time, allowing the opportunity for the two older children to forge a bond. Trevor became comfortable talking to the little girl.

Tiny voices would echo up the staircase from the basement playroom when the two were together. Julie was the first person to discover these little voices did not continue in her presence. Samantha had no trouble vocalizing in front of anyone, intelligibly or not, but Trevor began to stand out. His differences became more apparent as each day passed. Julie was met with silence and terrified expressions from the pale-faced four-year-old whenever she asked a question of him. She found herself using Samantha as the interpreter to determine things like which flavored snack he preferred.

Rag ball (like T-ball but for younger children) and soccer captured Trevor's interest at the young age of four. The organized sports allowed him to burn off some energy and frustration from the day's stresses. It was obvious Trevor didn't speak during practices, and the coaches appreciated this behavior, which they interpreted as respectful listening. But Julie questioned Trevor's quietness, bringing his uniqueness to the surface. Being made aware of this potential issue, I began to see there was indeed a problem.

During soccer practice one afternoon, I sat proudly in my unfolded chair along with all the other involved parents. We lined the edge of the soccer field like a game of red rover, chairs stretched side by side from one goal zone to the other. With our backs warming in the sun, we watched as our little loved ones kicked the ball around. They looked like a swarm of bees, following the lead bee with the ball. I spotted Trevor in the field behind the pack, picking clovers as if they were beautiful flowers. A little boy made his way over to Trevor's position and began talking. I heard his first question: "Whatcha got?" Extending his hand filled with limp greenery, Trevor answered the boy with a gesture. The encounter continued. "What are those, green flowers?" asked Trevor's new friend. Avoiding eye contact, Trevor shrugged his tiny shoulders, then returned to pick more "flowers." His little friend spotted a clover and clutched it in his grip as the ball rolled past them. With a command from the coach to "kick it," the two boys dropped their treasures and raced toward the rolling toy.

If Julie had not planted the seed of uncertainty, I might never have identified this incident as different. But it was obvious: Trevor was not using his voice.

PART 2

Life With Selective Mutism

CHAPTER 4

Diagnosing Selective Mutism

As summer came to an end, preparations for preschool began. Trevor was overjoyed about transitioning into a "big kid" going to school. Hope that he would be normal and talk to the other children was at the forefront of my thoughts. But from day one this was not the case. He remained silent the entire three hours of each class three days per week that preschool year.

After a couple of weeks into the new school year, Mrs. Gronefeld, the lead preschool teacher, asked me, "How do you get Trevor to talk to others?"

I'll never forget my impulsive reply. "When you figure that out, will you tell me?" Her surprised reaction immediately changed to doubt that Trevor could make any sound at all. I made it my quest to prove he did indeed speak at home by secretly recording him one evening. Hiding a small black tape recorder behind my purse on the table, I pressed the record button, then asked Trevor about his day. Without forethought I risked a sensitive question. "Do you like Mrs. Gronefeld?" The words spilled out of my mouth before I considered the implications of his possible responses. But luckily he did enjoy his preschool teacher and verbalized his affection for the bizarre woman on the tape recording. I took a breath of relief.

The following day I proudly toted the recording to the preschool. I played the tiny voice for both teachers to hear. Mrs. Gronefeld and her assistant, Mrs. Richmond, were in awe at the recording. They almost couldn't believe this silent child in class could sound so clear, confident, and strong. As his innocent yet confident voice played, their faces contorted in confusion. Neither had any inkling as to why he was so quiet outside the comfort of his home. Immediately they began to question if Trevor was being abused or traumatized in some manner to cause his strange mute behavior. This was not how I expected our impromptu meeting to go. My goal was to prove he *could* talk, not to create unfounded accusations against myself or our family. But their questions continued, probing deeper for answers. After a thorough examination they redirected their focus on the possibility of a traumatic event from earlier in his life causing Trevor's muteness. Both ladies were intrigued and agreed to do their own research on the matter.

When Trevor wasn't in preschool, he stayed at Julie's house. I attempted to shorten my workdays because he had separation anxiety. Trevor enjoyed playing at Julie's but still wanted me with him. His ideal day would have consisted of me staying at Julie's house so we could play together in her basement. This plan did not mesh with my work plan for obvious reasons. But try explaining it to a four-year-old!

Julie greeted me excitedly at the door one day when I arrived to pick up Trevor. She thrust a small piece of paper into my hand and eagerly explained the TV talk show she watched earlier. My heart raced in response to her heightened emotion. She had scribbled the topic of the day's show onto the paper, and glancing at the tiny note she had shoved into my palm, I read the messy scrawl which looked something like "sandnotes mints." My dumbfounded expression must have tamed her frenzy because she began pronouncing the written words slowly. S-e-l-e-c-t-i-v-e m-u-t-i-s-m. Trying to follow but lagging greatly, I asked her, "What is selective autism?"

"No, not autism, *mutism*," she answered. "I heard on the talk show that it's an anxiety disorder causing a child not to speak. So, I looked it up on the internet and read how typically a child with it doesn't talk in one or more settings for at least three months of their life."

Julie had done her homework, searching online for any report of the anxiety. With the limited information available during that decade, I was surprised she found any mention of the rare condition at all. Julie beamed with pride in her extraordinary discovery, declaring, "I think this is what Trevor has." I had to admit he *did* fit the profile she described.

The moment I arrived home, I dialed up the internet on my personal computer. Once connected, I began surfing the web for more details of this condition. In simple black and white were the words which changed our future. Selective mutism was real, and my child fit every requirement listed for a diagnosis. A quick call to Trevor's father convinced him a visit to a medical professional was necessary. We both shied away from giving our young son medication, so we focused on searching for child psychologists rather than psychiatrists, who might be more inclined to treat with drugs.

Relief was felt by the three of us the moment we realized we were alone in the waiting room of our new pediatric psychologist. Trevor immediately walked over to the toys on the table in the center of the room, and his father and I found chairs near the door. The vibrant colors in the room gave a joyful, juvenile atmosphere and eased our apprehension. It was a blessing no other people were in the room to spoil the calmness, but this was probably an intentional scheduling procedure.

We entered the specialist's office as a family unit. The thirty-something, slender man had a compassionate, gentle characteristic about him. His receding hairline gave the impression his job consumed him, adding years to his appearance. He spoke to the adults first. "What brings you in today?"

Trevor happily played at a Lego table nearby, appearing unaffected by the conversation. We're concerned our son is not using his voice when around other people, and we think it may be selective mutism," I answered. After giving a few examples of our silent child at preschool and with the babysitters, I mentioned Julie's discovery of the disorder.

"Hmm, selective mutism is quite rare," he replied skeptically. "I'll have to first rule out other possibilities before making a diagnosis." He then admitted he had never encountered the specific condition himself. After a brief, one-sided interview with Trevor, he asked to schedule a return visit so he could have more time with our child alone.

While awaiting a definitive answer to Trevor's issue, the next couple of weeks crept by so slowly it felt like months. The waiting game is never enjoyable and tested our patience. Finally D-day arrived, and we received a concrete diagnosis. Meeting the psychologist without Trevor present, he told us the news.

"Well, first off I believed Trevor had autism," he said, "so I focused on that problem and performed several tests before finally ruling it out. He is not autistic, although I thought he might be due to the way he avoids eye contact and interactions with others.

He continued, "I reached out to a couple of my colleagues because he didn't test positive for attention deficit disorder either, although he is borderline for hyperactivity. I believe the initial suggestion of selective mutism is the most accurate. Trevor fits all the signs and symptoms, so I am convinced this is the case. Corroboration with my colleagues has confirmed that diagnosis."

He continued to explain about a young patient with the same diagnosis one of his fellow therapists treated about six months ago. My thoughts drifted in response to the heightened emotion, causing my head to spin. Knowing for sure what was wrong with my child alleviated some stress. Now we had a definite diagnosis, and we could strategize a recovery plan. As my mind formulated a scenario of Trevor's journey to normalcy, I imagined he would be cured in about a month. Hearing the psychologist's prognosis startled me out of my wandering fantasy.

"So, I believe by the time Trevor is in third grade, around nine years of age, he'll be comfortable enough to speak in public."

"What? But he's only four right now. That's more than double his lifetime until he's cured," I exclaimed as the shock of this news defied my hopes for a quick recovery.

"As I said, there is no cure for selective mutism. He needs to mature and gain control over his anxieties to feel comfortable enough to use his voice around others." The doctor spoke slowly as if repeating a recent conversation, which I obviously did not comprehend. My mouth gaped open, unable to formulate any words to express my surprise and disappointment.

Trevor's father was more focused on why this disorder occurred, asking, "Did our divorce cause this problem?"

The psychologist immediately answered, "Doubtful, or else we would see many more cases. Since fifty percent of marriages end in divorce nowadays, more children would be displaying selective mutism symptoms." He followed up, "But that's not to say it didn't have some bearing on helping the disorder surface. The predisposition must already be present, and then a perceived trauma can contribute to the condition developing."

By the end of our meeting, fear and apprehension were consumed by acceptance. Trevor's father and I decided we would do whatever it took to help our young son learn to overcome this anxiety. He could beat this problem faster than expected with family support.

CHAPTER 5

Protective Momma Bear

After I informed the babysitter of the definitive diagnosis, she expressed mixed emotions. Julie was pleased her discovery of Trevor's selective mutism diagnosis was not erroneous, but she also worried about how to help in his recovery. I informed her of the suggestions given by the psychologist. The biggest recommendation was reducing focus on Trevor's lack of talking. The use of open-ended questions offered him an opportunity to speak. When he didn't respond verbally, we were instructed to accept his nonverbal gestures. Julie was excited about her role in his treatment plan. She was eager to help Trevor find his vocal path.

When I picked Trevor up from Julie's, she told me about an incident occurring earlier. Trevor decided Julie's downstairs walls were too bare for his liking and proceeded to add colorful crayon artwork. His little friend Samantha was eager to help in his quest to improve the décor. Together they colored to their hearts' content on Julie's basement walls. Unfortunately, Julie was less than enthusiastic about their design plan. But her fear of negatively impacting Trevor's anxiety prevented her from expressing her disappointment to him directly. I was quite upset this had occurred. I explained to Julie that Trevor does not get a free ride to hide behind his diagnosis. He must be disciplined like any other child. Calling him upstairs, I demanded Trevor apologize to Julie for his unacceptable behavior. With tears streaming down his little pink cheeks, Trevor faintly whispered "sorry" in Julie's direction. Glancing toward Julie, I discovered she, too, had tears streaming down her cheeks. The first word he had ever spoken to her created such a feeling of joy, all anger about his coloring mishap disappeared. Wiping her eyes, Julie babbled something about having Goo Gone and waved us out the door.

The preschool teachers graciously offered their support when informed of Trevor's condition. I did my best to educate everyone involved in his care so we would all be on the same page with the recovery plan. The most critical step in reducing his anxiety was to avoid bringing attention to Trevor. Even though he had not tried to speak in class, they began noticing small improvements in his demeanor. Trevor began making brief eye contact and played easily with the other children.

One sunny day at preschool the assistant teacher, Mrs. Richmond, approached me as I was walking Trevor into class. She smiled at Trevor and wished him a good morning. He returned the smile, then raced to the check-in board to turn his name card over, displaying his attendance. Mrs. Richmond spoke to me privately. "I want to give Trevor one of my hand puppets. I'm hoping it'll encourage him to talk through the puppet, maybe take the pressure off of him. But I wanted to run it past you first." I loved the idea and enthusiastically gave her my blessing.

Later that afternoon I pulled my car into the pickup line outside the preschool. Parked behind all the other eager parents, I awaited my child. My windshield displayed the orange paper card with Trevor's name, indicating to whom I belonged. The color represented Mrs. Gronefeld's class. As her scout spotted orange cards, he would call out the listed names. After hearing a loud "Trevor," Mrs. Gronefeld grabbed my son's hand and headed toward our vehicle. Dangling out of Trevor's school pail was a fuzzy lion. My smile widened with excitement when I spotted his new puppet. While Trevor climbed into the back of our car, Mrs. Gronefeld buckled him into his seat and wished him a good day. As she closed the door, they waved their farewells to one another through the glass.

Trevor's excitement bubbled over. First, he grabbed his artwork, proudly holding it up for me to view. Then, he held up the puppet. "This is Leo the Lion; Mrs. Richmond gave it to me."

"Leo the Lion, that's cute. Why did she give you a puppet?" I asked as innocently as I could muster.

With a little shrug from his tiny shoulders, he replied, "I don't know. She said he can't talk and wanted me to keep him until he finds his voice." Tossing the lion puppet on the seat next to the discarded artwork, he began rooting through his pail again, searching for more objects of importance. The car line started moving, and soon it was our turn to exit the parking lot, heading for home.

Trevor continued to show me the contents of his pail from the back seat. Holding up each item for me to view, I glanced in the rearview mirror to see his prized trinkets of the day. After he was satisfied I had witnessed each object, he placed the pail onto the seat next to him. Occasionally I heard a thud as his treasures rolled off the seat onto the floorboard. Driving home was fun that day, hearing about finger-paint time, how Jack dressed up in a princess costume during free-play, and, of course, the puppet. His little hand struggled to move the lion's mouth, so it looked more like the lion's nose was speaking. But it was cute nonetheless.

Leo the Lion lived in our house that entire preschool year, unable to speak outside of the home. Just before summer I asked Mrs. Richmond if she wanted him back. She declined. "Let him keep him, maybe it'll still work in time, and he'll be able to talk through the puppet," she declared with a hopeful voice. I had my doubts, but it was a sweet gesture and a creative idea.

The summer was filled with extended silence from Trevor and Leo, neither being able to talk in public. I continued encouraging Trevor to speak, following the recommendation to not focus attention on his lack of voice. One visit to the psychologist's office was disconcerting. Trevor, his father, and I were in the waiting room, awaiting his appointment. We had the room to ourselves as usual, and Trevor was feeling brave. He chatted quite confidently with both of us. Abruptly the psychologist opened the door and announced, "I heard you talking, Trevor, and nothing bad happened." The unexpected sharp words stung and caused Trevor's face to blanch of color and his eyes to widen in terror. Watching our young son retreat in fear, once again hiding behind my legs, generated anger toward this man. He did what he advised us against; he brought attention to Trevor using his voice. Needless to say, that was our last visit with this medical professional. The setback took about a month for Trevor to recover from, and he was more guarded whenever we were alone in public, keeping his conversations to a whisper.

My protective mom mode kicked in again at the pediatric dentist's office later that summer. Trevor's selective mutism diagnosis was previously explained to the dentist, and it was written in his chart to not force him to speak. At one visit Trevor was taken back for a routine cleaning. The office rule did not allow parents to go back with their children, not even a child with an anxiety disorder. The whole room was tailored to kids, with colorful little furniture everywhere you looked. Trevor had been to this office before and managed well, so I did not anticipate any issues. Unfortunately, as Trevor returned from his cleaning, he was silently crying. *What the heck?* I leaned down so he could whisper into my ear out of view from the office staff. His timid voice quivered. "The lady wouldn't let me point to bubble gum flavor." Sniffling back a sob, he finally managed to continue, "She said if I didn't say which flavor I wanted, she would mix the two and it would be yucky." The fact that cherry, bubblegum, or a combination of the two flavors probably tasted equally yucky was irrelevant. The dental hygienist ignored the note in his chart about his diagnosis, which was the only relevant issue. I was furious, and everyone in that office and the waiting room heard how furious. Did I overreact? Possibly—ok, probably—but who can control "mom mode" when your baby is being attacked? Sure, *attacked* might be a slight exaggeration, but controlling the emotional roller coaster can be challenging once set in motion. Trevor wasn't exactly happy when I stuck up for him. He kept pulling on my leg to flee the situation altogether. The attention I had brought upon us was probably worse for Trevor than the initial injustice. Even though my heart (but not necessarily my mouth) was in the right place, I realized later it was not the best reaction for my anxious child. What is it they say about hindsight?

CHAPTER 6

Fighting Fear with Fear

Preparing Trevor for the upcoming kindergarten screening was our next biggest obstacle. I knew Trevor would be required to use his voice. For two weeks I mentally prepared him for what to expect, describing in detail what I recalled from his brother's screening four years prior. Trevor's excited desire to attend big-kid school motivated him and helped reduce the dreaded fear of speaking. My own fears grew as each day passed, and I worried his eagerness would not be enough to overcome his anxiety. Trevor had not been able to use his voice in public with a stranger up to this point, so this kindergarten screening would be a huge obstacle for him.

I tried to reduce Trevor's embarrassment about talking aloud by not focusing on using his voice during the kindergarten screening. But his lack of speech was the only issue that might prevent him from passing the interview. How do you prepare a child to use their voice without commenting on the need to use their voice? It was an impossible position. Without saying "You must *talk* to the interviewer," I instead focused on an indirect approach. Using his fear of not being accepted into kindergarten, I simplified the situation for Trevor. "If you don't answer the questions, you can't go to kindergarten." To soften the blow, I quickly followed up with

"They will have no idea how smart you are unless you answer their questions." This explanation reduced the emphasis on his actual speech.

Apprehension followed me during those days leading up to the kindergarten screening. My stomach felt like it housed a swarm of butterflies, spawning an uncontrollable nausea. I was unsure if my approach—using Trevor's fear of not attending kindergarten to persuade him to overcome his fear of speaking—would help or hinder. But I decided the only way to beat fear was with a greater fear. If Trevor genuinely wanted to go to kindergarten, then the fear of not going would be greater than the fear of using his voice. My hypothesis would be proven or disproven soon enough.

On the day of the kindergarten screening, I was a nervous wreck. Trevor was a bit pale, but he seemed confident. Continuing my encouragement in preparation for his exam, I reminded him the interview was a test for his school readiness. I explained to my young son, "We both know you are very ready for school; you simply have to prove it to the teacher." Trevor's little nod indicated he understood.

We entered the front office of the elementary school. The receptionist directed us down the hall to another room assigned for the kindergarten screenings. In that room there was a small waiting area with two chairs and a bookshelf filled with picture books. We each sat and waited for Trevor's turn. I smiled warmly to my nervous child, hiding my own heightened anxiety. His wide eyes glowed with emotion, but before I could determine his mental status, the interviewer opened her office door. She made a brief introduction, then guided Trevor back, closing the door behind him. The moment passed by in a blur. Fear struck as I sat there, worried I hadn't uttered a single warning to the teacher about his problem.

Staring at the closed door, I felt helpless to guide my son. It might as well have been the Berlin Wall dividing us, making me feel countries apart. Trevor was on his own. All I could do was pray, which I did fervently. The second hand on the clock hanging above my head seemed to be in a time warp, slowing its movement with each click echoing through the room. My head began to spin. Inhaling deeply, I felt my chest rise. Exhaling slowly, I focused on regaining control and shaking off the stress. I wondered what Trevor must be feeling. If my body was responding so powerfully to the moment, how was his little body reacting? Thinking about my scared son, my eyes burned, and tears threatened to spill over my reddened lids.

Suddenly the door opened. I expected to see my child silently crying, having failed the interview. But what I saw was contradicting. Trevor was smiling! The interaction between the teacher and my anxiety-ridden child did not compute. Mrs. Powell, the kindergarten interviewer, waved to my little boy and said, "I'll see you in a couple of weeks, Trevor. Enjoy the rest of your summer." I was confused.

"I, um, how did he do?" I finally managed to squeak.

"He did great. He's ready for kindergarten, no problems," answered Mrs. Powell as Trevor beamed with pride.

"Oh, that's wonderful," I responded with relief. "So, he . . . answered your questions . . . ok?" I probed, only wanting to know if he used his voice. But since Trevor was listening, I didn't draw attention to his verbal abilities directly.

"Yes, he answered everything appropriately. Like I said, he's ready to start school." Mrs. Powell replied with slight irritation, confused as to why I couldn't comprehend her statement the first time.

"Oh, ok, I was merely concerned because he was recently diagnosed with selective mutism," I stated to clarify my initial reaction.

"Yes, I saw that written in his chart, but he gave no indication to worry and answered each question clearly. I don't anticipate any problems this school year." Mrs. Powell replied with a finality in her voice, which told me our conversation was over. I got the impression she enjoyed young people more than adults. But I suppose dealing with stressful parents might've been a swaying factor.

Trevor and I were overjoyed with the outcome of his screening but for different reasons. He was proud of being accepted into kindergarten. I was astonished he had spoken in front of a stranger. In the car I tried to determine how much Trevor used his voice during the interview. Choosing my words carefully, I asked, "What did you

31

say when she asked you who lived in our house?" repeating one of the questions I recalled from Josh's interview.

"I told her the truth," he answered. "My brother, mom, step-dad, and our two cats." Trevor described the simple shapes she had him draw and various other areas of interest. Then he questioned me. "Why are you asking me so much. Didn't you think I would pass?"

His dejected words hung in the air for a moment. "Oh no, sweetie, I know you're smart, but I was worried the teacher might not see how intelligent you are," I sputtered, trying to recover from his hurtful response. Then I explained to my son about test anxiety. "When I was younger, I didn't always do well when I was nervous. I was afraid that might happen to you too."

His concerns lifted, and he nodded in acceptance. "Nope, not me, I didn't have any problems." His response and sweet smile warmed my heart. I was proud of my baby for overcoming his fear and using his voice in front of a stranger.

CHAPTER 7

A Milestone: First Day of Kindergarten

The day before school started, we attended an open house. All the chairs were so tiny and colorful, perfect for the little bodies who would inhabit them soon. Each child was assigned a cubby and hook for placing their belongings. Individual nametags were on the desks, also assigning each child with a specific seat. I spotted Mrs. Powell at the front of the room, greeting the children and enduring their parents. As Trevor wandered around, looking at all the colorful posters and displays, I made my way up front to join the line to speak with the teacher. She had a forced smile on her face, which didn't quite reach her eyes. I could tell she would rather be anywhere than here dealing with these demanding adults. Finally, it was my turn; I stepped forward to talk. I felt it was important to remind the teacher about Trevor's issues, so I proceeded to explain. The moment I mentioned "He's afraid to use his voice in front of strangers," Mrs. Powell interjected.

"Trevor had no problems during our interview, and he did not indicate fear of using his voice. I anticipate he will be just fine."

She continued with slight irritation as if she had given a variation of this speech at least a dozen times tonight. "Parents always worry about their child's first day of kindergarten, but I think the adults are more fearful. From my experience the kids are happily excited. Let's see how the first couple of days go, and if any issues arise, I will be sure to contact you." She offered a strained smile, then turned to the next set of parents with needless concerns. My eyebrows raised in surprise at her indifference. But she has more than twenty years' experience, I thought, so she must know what she's doing. I decided to put my faith in her abilities.

The next morning when we stood at the bus stop near the boys' father's house was one of the hardest moments of my life. The air buzzed with excitement, and Trevor and Josh eagerly awaited the upcoming bus ride. The anticipated first day at school was the topic of their discussion. My nerves were raw, and I was preoccupied with concern for Trevor's mental health while away. I said a silent prayer that he would be alright. Knowing his brother would be nearby in the school did provide some comfort. Suddenly Josh cried out, "Here comes the bus!" I glanced toward the end of the road and watched the large yellow vehicle turn onto the street. At that exact moment I felt a sharp sting in the back of my knee. Tears collected in my eyes in response to the pain the bee inflicted.

Trevor's dad noticed my expression and reacted comfortingly. "I know how you're feeling; it's hard, watching our babies grow up." There was no time to explain the true reason for my tears. The bus had pulled up, and the door opened. Quick hugs were given to both children, and then I watched as they climbed the stairs and chose their seats. They sat together, waving at us from their window.

Stifling back a grimace from the pain in my knee, I forced a loving smile and blew them kisses. Snatching the imaginary kiss from the air, they each shoved their whimsical prize into their pockets for later. Then we waved an "I love you" in American Sign Language (ASL). That was our thing, catching kisses and signing our love whenever we parted. Each boy responded accordingly with his little hand, folding down the two middle fingers and extending the other digits into the sign, indicating they loved me too. The burning behind my knee increased tenfold with every second that passed. How could one little stinger cause so much discomfort? At this point the tears freely flowed down my cheeks, but I stood my ground and provided the visual memory of happy parents watching and waving as they rode off to their destiny. The moment the bus was out of sight, I grabbed for my leg and screamed out in pain. My ex-husband was surprised but soon realized the reason for my outburst. He quickly fetched an ice pack from inside his house before he left for work. I sat on his steps and held the ice in place, now crying emotional tears. I'm unsure how long I sat there a blubbering, sobbing mess. By the time I left, the throbbing in my knee had subsided; only the fear of Trevor's selective mutism remained.

Focusing on work was difficult while the boys were at school their first day. My thoughts drifted to Trevor, and I imagined how his day was unfolding. One moment I imagined Trevor using his voice like every other child, then the next I envisioned him silently crying in a corner, unnoticed. This emotional rollercoaster was exhausting, and I couldn't wait for the day to come to an end. Either outcome would be better than not knowing. Finally, I finished work and raced to the bus stop to collect my boys.

After scouting the immediate area for pain-inducing bees, I determined it safe enough to avert my attention to watch for the bus. Not surprisingly, it was a few minutes late. The first week was always off schedule, conceivably due to concerned parents monopolizing the bus driver's time at each stop. I made a mental note not to be one of those parents.

My stomach felt like a net full of butterflies as I watched the bus pull up. Desperately searching through the windows for my little men, I spotted two heads popping up between the tall seats near the aisle. I waved to the bus driver and offered a warm smile. Trevor was the first one to negotiate the steps, wearing a huge grin that stretched from ear to ear. I raced over to help him down the final big step. He waved my hand away in a display of independence. Instead of stepping, he opted for hopping off the bus with Josh close behind.

Trevor gave the impression day one of kindergarten was fun, but that wasn't the pressing issue. Did he manage to speak in class as he did during his interview? Finding the right words to determine if he used his voice was a delicate matter. I decided to ease into it and posed a general question about how their day went. Both boys responded with "great." Josh provided many details about who was in his fourth grade class and how he already had homework. Trevor excitedly described a couple of his classmates, too, mimicking his brother's response. He then exclaimed, "I also have homework."

"No, you don't," argued Josh. "They don't give homework in kindergarten."

"I do too!" insisted Trevor, and he proceeded to pull out papers from his backpack to prove his claim.

"Ok, ok. Let's go home, and we'll go through everything. You don't want any of your papers to fly away in the wind," I said. Trevor shoved his contents back into his backpack, then walked to our car parked nearby. The two boys quickly recovered from their disagreement, blithely chatting together while climbing into the backseat of the car.

After Josh shared the details of his day, he gave me the medical information packet and various necessary parental forms. I turned my focus to Trevor. He handed me a stack of crinkled papers, which he had hastily shoved into his book bag. There was a homework packet hidden within the mess he provided. To gain an understanding of each child's academic level, the kindergarten teacher included various questions in the homework packet. Included were simple math, reading, and color identification problems. Since the kindergarteners could not read, I realized this homework focused on parental involvement. My mind began to paint a clearer picture of Mrs. Powell. I had to admit the woman was growing on me. She encouraged parental interaction with the kids from day one. This homework assignment provided me the perfect time to inquire about Trevor's day.

"So, did you meet any new friends in your class today?" I asked nonchalantly.

"Yea, I met Chase and Nicholas. They were funny," replied my sweet child.

"Oh, Nicholas, that's the same name as our Nick," I acknowledged, referring to my soon-to-be husband.

Trevor's nose wrinkled, and he contested my statement. "No, his name is Nicholas, not Nick."

I explained how Nick is short for Nicholas. Offering another example, I mentioned how Josh is short for Joshua. This piqued his interest, but he soon discovered he was left out of the nickname group. I quickly offered appeasement and reminded him that he did indeed have a nickname. Sometimes I called him Trev for short. This satisfied his concerns, and he began chatting about his other new friend, Chase.

Eventually I worked in a strategic question. "Did you tell Chase or Nicholas about your family or pets?"

"No." His simple response left more unanswered questions in my mind. I knew I had to be delicate with my phrasing, but I longed to know if he spoke.

"Did you tell them anything at all about you, or did they only talk about themselves?" I pried.

"They talked about themselves mostly but also about stuff in class. They're nice and funny." With his final comment failing to answer my underlying question about using his voice, I decided it might be easier to ask his teacher. Trevor was a smart boy, and he would be alerted if I continued to pry. I decided to drop the subject and focus on his homework.

The next day I used the volunteer sign-up as an excuse to speak with Trevor's teacher before class. I volunteered for the four years Josh spent in elementary school, so Trevor was not suspicious of my visit with his teacher. It is important to be open and informative with children to reduce their stress and anxiety.

Arriving early that morning, I knocked on the open door frame of Mrs. Powell's classroom. The moment she made eye contact, I noticed a flash of disappointment that I was an adult and not a child. I offered my services to help with her needs on my days off. Initially she declined, mumbling something about high school students helping soon. But my perseverance won, and she agreed to allow me to visit each Wednesday. Yes, my foot was in the door!

Contemplating how to approach her with my concerns about Trevor, Mrs. Powell broke my wandering thoughts. "By the way, Trevor did not speak in class yesterday. I know he has an anxiety disorder, so I let him slide. But I require each child to respond when I do roll call. He must let me know he is present."

My heart sank as my fears swelled inside my chest. There it was, the answer to my question. Not the answer I had hoped for, but at least now I knew. Trevor was not talking in class; he had not managed to overcome his selective mutism.

"I will talk to him tonight and emphasize the importance of answering you when called upon." I quickly added, "But his doctor said we should not force him to talk before he is ready."

"If he continues to have verbal issues, you may need to request an IEP," Mrs. Powell said.

"What's an IEP?" I asked, confused.

"It's an educational plan to help children with disabilities or to assign them to an adult chaperone assistant to help him communicate," she explained.

The word *disability* hung in the air for what seemed like several minutes. This is something I never considered my child to have—a disability. It was a hard word to accept. Mrs. Powell's impatience grew at my silence. "Oh, I would rather not go that route," I finally mustered.

"Yes, I agree, but he should respond when I call out his name," she asserted. I begged for her patience to allow adjustment time. She agreed to overlook his resistance, stating, "Kindergarten is about learning the foundation of formal education and establishing social interactions. I will give him time to become accustomed to our routines."

After dinner that evening I had a heart-to-heart with my bambino. "I saw Mrs. Powell today and offered to volunteer each week. She said it was ok to check if she needs any help. Would you like it if I popped into your class?"

"Yea, that'd be cool," replied Trevor. He continued coloring in his book.

"Great, it would be fun to see you too. By the way, Mrs. Powell said she has a rule in her class. Everyone must answer when she calls their name. Did you know about this rule?"

"Yea, I know, she told me I had to say hi. She really wants me to say, 'Hi, Mrs. Powell,' but she said I could just say hi."

"Did you say hi today when she called your name?"

I was met with silence from my child. He stared intently at the picture he was coloring, then finally responded. "I tried, but it's hard."

"I'm sure it's scary for everyone, being in a new class with new people," I said sympathetically. "But Mrs. Powell said if you can't answer when she calls, you might need an adult to sit with you during school. Someone who can help you communicate," I explained.

This piqued Trevor's interest, and his expression almost looked excited. "Really? Would you be the one to sit with me?" He asked enthusiastically.

"No babe, not me. It has to be one of the workers at the school."

His little face scrunched in a scowl, and he answered, "I don't want anyone to sit with me. That would be weird."

"I agree, I wouldn't like it either. But that doesn't have to happen if you start answering Mrs. Powell in class. Just say hi like she asked. It's important to follow rules in school."

Trevor contemplated my statement, then nodded in acceptance. I wasn't sure if the fear of having a stranger next to him was bigger than the fear of saying hi in front of the class. Time would tell.

CHAPTER 8

The Impact of Togetherness

The next morning arrived too quickly. Trevor, Josh, and I had difficulty adjusting to the early school schedule. The hands on the clock revealed how late we had run that morning. There wasn't enough time to drive to the bus stop near the boys' father's house, but I was determined to try because I knew how much Trevor enjoyed riding the bus. Quickly I grabbed all my work items and shouted out commands: "Get your shoes," "Grab your backpack," and "Here, eat this cereal bar." We finally piled into the car and began our frantic and futile drive to the bus stop. As we turned onto the road, I saw the bus rolling past the empty stop, continuing its journey to the next group of kids. Darn it, they missed the bus.

Using the free time the boys would have spent on the bus, we visited a nearby park with an Indian burial mound. This park was a highlight of our city. The 113 steps to the top of the mound felt like fifteen miles when I attempted to negotiate them as quickly as my two young, energetic boys. I avoided appearing weak (or old) in front of my children by ascending the huge flight with feigned ease. The burning in my thighs screamed for me to stop, but watching Josh and Trevor run ahead gave me the motivation to persevere. Especially as they both raced up to the platform and turned to watch dear old mother struggle behind. The moment my foot cleared the final step, it was time to leave for school. After a hurried view of the scenic sight on the top of the mound, the three of us raced down the steps toward the parking lot. I descended the staircase much more easily than I climbed, but my lungs struggled from the exertion nonetheless.

The car seemed to move farther away with every step I took. My legs threatened to give out at any moment. Finally, we made it back, and I rushed to unlock the door. My body collapsed into the seat. I slid the key into the ignition, then discovered my muscles were too exhausted to push in the clutch. I mentally cursed my decision to buy a stick shift.

Josh questioned my procrastination. "I thought you said we had to leave now, or we'd be late?" At this statement it was time to admit the reason for my delay. I explained to the boys how my legs were too tired to drive. That did not compute since they only saw my arms doing all the work, steering when I drove. After a few minutes of Josh and Trevor brainstorming ideas on how to make the car drive with the two of them pushing on the pedals, I finally tapped into some stored muscle energy. That was the most difficult four-minute drive I can ever remember. Half of the time I had to use one hand pushing my leg and the other on the steering wheel. As soon as I entered the parking lot, I pulled into the closest space, rather than entering the drop-off circle, to save more energy. The boys jumped out and exchanged our typical "I love you" ASL sign, then disappeared through the door into the school building. It took another ten minutes for my legs to fully recover to drive away. During this time I pulled out my cell phone and pretended to talk so no one would think I was a weird, creepy lady stalking young children at the school.

Later that day when we were home, I questioned Trevor on whether he used his voice in school. While he played happily with his cars and trucks on his rug printed with city roads, I delicately approached him with the question. "Trevor, sweetie, did you follow Mrs. Powell's rule this morning when she called your name?"

Trevor continued to push his truck around on the road of his floor mat. His lack of reply led me to believe he hadn't heard me. So, I decided to try again.

"Sweetie, did you say hi to Mrs. Powell today in school like she wanted?"

Again I was met with silence.

"You know you have to follow her rules, right, like all the other kids?"

At this further probing Trevor became visibly upset and crashed his toy truck into the parked cars nearby. Then, he stood up, screamed incoherently, and threw the truck across the room, hitting his toy box. The truck bounced off and flew back in our direction, grazing his leg as he passed. Trevor's anger increased. He stomped his feet and kicked the truck as punishment for hitting his leg, then stormed out of the room. I stood there, shocked at his sudden outburst. Obviously I had provoked him, but there was no warning. Directness was not the answer for handling him now, and regret filled me as I contemplated how to proceed.

"Trevor, throwing your toys is not acceptable behavior!" I shouted toward his small disappearing outline.

This caused him to scream louder as he ran down the hallway. The moment he entered his room, he slammed the door. Our conversation was over.

CHAPTER 9

Giant Leap of Progress

Week two of school and my first volunteer day arrived. Trevor was still delighted when he rode the school bus, but he also expressed excitement when he rode in the car with me as he did that morning. He held my hand as we entered the building together. Having an older son, I knew this public affection would not last long, so I savored the moment. Josh was content to walk alone.

I gave each boy a warm hug, and then we parted at the front office entrance. We waved our "I love you" signs to one another as we headed in our separate directions. The boys lined up with their cooresponding grade in the hallway awaiting the bell. I signed the volunteer book and obtained a pass to walk past the office and toward the classrooms. Josh's teacher was first on my radar for helping, so off I headed to the fourth grade hall.

After copies were made, I ventured toward Mrs. Powell's room at the opposite end of the building. The redheaded teacher spotted me quickly the moment I popped my head into her doorway. Amazingly, she smiled. And more amazingly, it was a warm, compassionate smile. The children were busy coloring at their desks, oblivious to my intrusion. Mrs. Powell made her way over to me and asked, "I hope you are here to help?"

"Yes, anything you need," I conceded eagerly.

"Great, I have a few papers I need copied. But I need them on special colored paper, so let me get those for you." She returned to the front of the room and opened drawers from her desk as she searched for the colored paper.

I glanced around the room, then spotted my sweet boy bravely smiling up at me. I blew him a kiss, then heard the boy next to him ask, "Trevor, is that your mom?" Trevor's face turned red in reaction to being singled out, but he nodded at his friend, agreeing. Even though the focus was on Trevor, he maintained his smile. He survived that social interaction, and I was proud. It was a small accomplishment, but the value was huge.

Mrs. Powell returned with packs of blue and yellow paper and provided directions on which color to use with the corresponding handout. After she finished guiding me, I asked, "Has Trevor talked at all in class?"

"No, he has not attempted to use his voice," she replied. "But in time maybe he will come around."

"Do we have to get an IEP since he's not talking?" I asked fearfully.

"We can pursue that possibility later. I'm hoping it doesn't come to that, but it's always an option," she admitted. "Sometimes, once a child has an adult answering for them, they become less likely to overcome their issues on their own. I'm concerned Trevor may not talk at all if someone is there to communicate for him. Let's wait and see what happens."

I offered a weak smile in response, but my eyes flooded with doubt. If Mrs. Powell couldn't get him to talk with her authoritarian personality, then I was unsure if anyone could. But it was early in the school year; we still had plenty of time. I decided to accept her perspective.

The next couple of months passed with little change in Trevor's anxiety or verbal skills. While this may not appear as improvement, I viewed it positively. Factoring in our unexpected family stresses, it was amazing Trevor had not regressed.

One evening after work I totaled my car in a head-on collision. My life was spared, but our family car was not. This directly impacted our routine. Trevor thrived on sameness, but life was no longer the same. Due to my sprained ankle I had to walk on crutches—more than an inconvenience as I was now unable to drive a stick shift. But the optimist in me deduced fortune was on my side. The replacement vehicle was an automatic. Therefore, I still drove Josh and Trevor to school and sports.

One evening Trevor and I attended Josh's soccer game. I hobbled from the parking lot to the soccer field as quickly as my crutches allowed, which could be compared to the speed of a turtle crossing a road. As I lugged two folding chairs on my back and a crutch in each hand, Trevor struggled with my slow pace. He ran ahead several feet, then stopped to wait on gimpy mom. His priceless expression spoke volumes in one impatient scowl. He stood facing me, shoulders slouched forward and eyes expressing utter frustration. Finally, we made it to the sideline, and I unfolded our chairs. Exhausted, I plopped myself into the seat and rubbed my hands together to be rid of the discomfort from the crutches.

Josh was already on the field, having been dropped off earlier for practice. It was Trevor and me hanging out together. While that gave the perfect opportunity for bonding, it was also a challenge to keep an energetic five-year-old entertained for an hour. Trevor did not enjoy "watching" other children play. He needed to experience the activity himself. Often I reminded him that during his soccer games their roles were reversed. Josh had to sit and watch him play. This explanation satisfied him for about thirty seconds. The other fifty-nine minutes and thirty seconds were hell on earth. Even though he brought his favorite toys, they did not offer much reprieve. After a typical meltdown with Trevor kicking and squirming, he ended up with his chair flipped on its side. While he pulled up grass and tossed it over his newly formed chair wall, he buried the discarded toys.

After he finished his grassy fun and set his chair upright, Trevor decided he wanted candy. The boys earned a weekly allowance, a recent initiative I started by giving them fifty cents per every year old they were. Trevor had two dollars and fifty cents burning a hole in his pocket. Unfortunately, being on crutches posed a logistical issue for me. I glanced across the field near the parking lot at the concession stand. It was probably a hundred feet away. I needed the game time to recover before having to walk again with my crutches. But Trevor was oblivious to my physical exhaustion. He begged for candy. Suddenly an opportunity unfolded. It was the perfect chance for Trevor to try to talk in public. So, I chose my words carefully and offered another option for my child.

"I am so sore from walking with my crutches, sweetie, that I simply can't make it over to the concession stand. But I will watch you while you go and buy your candy."

"I can go by myself?" Trevor asked apprehensively.

"Yes, but I won't take my eyes off you the whole time. I can see you from here—I'll even wave whenever you look back so you'll know I'm watching," I said reassuringly.

Trevor nodded in acceptance of the proposition and trudged off toward the concession stand, money stowed in his front pocket. I did as I promised and watched him the whole way. Panic suddenly struck. What had I done? My innocent little boy ventured into the world alone. If anything happened, I couldn't run to him. I couldn't save him. My chest felt heavy as Trevor approached the concession stand window. I held my breath and watched helplessly. He turned in my direction, and my hand shot up in a frantic wave, nearly coaxing him to return. His little hand gestured a small wave back, and then he changed his focus to the candy display inside the small building. The lady in the concession stand leaned forward out the window and peered down at the small figure. I was too far away to hear the verbal exchange, but it appeared that Trevor used words to place his order. The lady disappeared into the concession stand briefly and returned with his candy and change. He did it. He actually did it! My jaw dropped open in disbelief. His return walk was much slower than his route over. Trevor was too distracted by his candy consumption to care about speed. Now I was the impatient one as I awaited his arrival. I wanted to know everything, every little detail of the exchange. Was he able to verbalize his candy order request, or did he settle with whatever candy the worker offered? I knew Trevor's anxiety would be triggered if I was too intrusive. So, when he finally arrived at our chairs, I started with a simple question.

"What kind of candy did you tell the lady you wanted?"

Shoving his half-eaten Kit Kat bar in my direction, Trevor proudly displayed his accomplishment.

"Oh, you asked her for a Kit Kat?" I inquired.

He glanced at me with surprised eyes. Even though he probably wondered why the lady would give him something other than what he ordered, he offered an agreeable nod and climbed into his chair. I was so proud of him at that moment but worried about causing a setback. I targeted my excitement toward his physical journey of walking alone to the concession stand.

"I'm so proud of you for walking all by yourself and facing your fears to get your candy." His chocolatey smile melted my heart. Today was a giant leap in his progress toward overcoming selective mutism.

CHAPTER 10

Using Anger as an Outlet

The months passed by in a blur. Trevor was still unsuccessful in using his voice in kindergarten, but he socialized in his own way. The other children enjoyed his presence, so he was fortunate in that aspect. More than a dozen kids showed up for his birthday party. They stood arm in arm and showered him with hugs. Somehow Trevor drew people in without any verbal skills. Even though other children seemed to enjoy his presence, Trevor still appeared as an outsider who watched the world from a distance. My heart yearned for him to step out of the shadows and find enough comfort to speak with his friends.

Summer is always an exciting time for children. School is out, which disrupts their normal routines. But the possibility of sleeping in, playing all day, and simply hanging out with friends is enticing. Too bad us adults can't follow that same schedule and take the whole summer off from life's responsibilities. But for most of us, adulting continues even into the summer months. That meant finding a reliable, trustworthy babysitter was crucial. Fortunately for us, we found Julie when Trevor was entering preschool. Luckily she was still in the babysitting business for another summer. The relief in knowing our boys were in safe, loving hands was immeasurable. Especially with having a child suffering from selective mutism.

Everyone's emotions were heightened at the end of the academic year. Trevor was no exception. After he bottled up his frustrations from maintaining silence throughout the entire school day, he typically unloaded on the return journey. There are permanent imprints of Trevor's feet from all the stomping during his meltdown moments in the car. There was no distraction big enough to prevent these outbursts. To dissuade his hostile reaction, I turned on light music and redirected focus to Josh. This tactic seemed most beneficial for allowing Trevor time to calm down and de-stress. If I asked him many questions, it threw him into a temper tantrum any two-year-old would be proud to claim.

One afternoon Trevor kicked the back of Josh's seat and screamed incoherently, but Josh had grown tired of Trevor's chosen outlet.

"Why do you let Trevor carry on like that? If I did even half of what he's doing, I'd have my Gameboy taken away for a week."

He had a good point, but I was afraid to admit it aloud. Trevor was gradually making progress toward opening up in school. I didn't want to chance a regression.

"Sweetie, your brother is under a lot of stress during the day. He's younger than you, so he hasn't learned any other way of dealing with his anger." I attempted to explain, unsure if I was trying to convince Josh or myself.

"Just because he has selective mutism, doesn't mean he should get special treatment," Josh stated in an agitated tone.

"Actually, it does. I'm sorry it doesn't seem fair to you. But Trevor must learn how to deal with his anxiety. So, until he has a better handle on it, he needs an outlet. Screaming and kicking seem to be the only thing helping him release his immediate frustrations after holding it in all day at school. But hopefully we'll find a better method for next school year. I promise to try harder to help him learn better coping techniques."

Josh nodded in agreement, apparently appeased with the prospect that next school year might be better. At this point I couldn't imagine it much worse.

The angry outbursts often lasted into the evening, but outside of the confines of the car, Trevor's temper wasn't as severe. Drawing was a productive outlet, and he was quite a good artist. His creativity, combining colors and patterns, made beautiful collages of abstract art worthy of framing. I hung one on my wall, which remains years after it was created. Trevor's love for art made complete sense to me. His artistic talents were enhanced because of his anxiety, and he used art as his expressive medium instead of sound. The emotions had to seep out one way or another, and art was more constructive than broken car seats. Unfortunately, Trevor was unable to simply jump into the car and draw. This anger-relieving method only worked after he released some of the pent-up anxieties from the day. He needed to calm down enough to be redirected appropriately. It didn't stop me from having conversations with him about his anger, but my timing had to be strategized. Living with a child who suffers from anxieties was like walking on eggshells. I had to skirt the path carefully and tactfully without crushing his spirit or triggering his emotions.

One evening I made Trevor's favorite dinner of chicken and dumplings. An opportunity presented itself for us to have a chat.

"Hey, babe, hope you liked your dumplings tonight."

"Yea, they were yummy, thanks," Trevor replied appreciatively.

"It makes me sad to see you suffer so much with your anger, not having a better way to express yourself." I chose my words cautiously, hopeful not to trigger his temper. "So, I was thinking maybe you could try some deep breathing when you feel really upset. Here, let me show you." I proceeded to breathe in through my nose and out through my mouth—slowly, steadily with closed eyes.

Initially Trevor thought the breathing technique was silly to try when he wasn't angry. But he finally conceded and gave it an attempt.

After he completed one deep inhale followed by a long exhale, he announced, "Ok, I'll try that if I get angry."

I snickered at the word *if*, which caused Trevor to glare in my direction. "I'm sorry, sweetie, but you said *if* you get angry. Everyone gets angry; it's a part of life. So, it's more like *when* you get angry," I explained calmly.

"Oh, right, that's true." He agreed, then returned to playing with his playdough.

The interaction gave me an uplifting feeling of hope. Maybe he would learn to control this anxiety-induced anger. Time would tell.

Trevor's kindergarten teacher, Mrs. Powell, confided to me she was moving up a grade next school year and planned to teach first grade. She advised that if I wanted Trevor to have her as his teacher, I must write a petition. Generally they did not honor requests for specific teachers, but with Trevor's diagnosis we stood a good chance of this request being granted. My weekly involvement with volunteering also had a positive impact.

Mrs. Powell's main reason for changing to first grade was a personal preference. The secondary benefit of helping Trevor was a bonus. I felt strongly that Trevor would flourish in her classroom next year if given the chance. Since his anxiety was triggered by unfamiliar settings, having the same teacher would help reassure him and reduce unnecessary stress. He might even progress to using his voice, although his psychologist's words replayed in my head. "I believe by the time Trevor is in third grade, around nine years of age, he'll be comfortable enough to speak in public." But that was one man's hypothesis. He could've been wrong. I believed Mrs. Powell would be the best choice for Trevor's first grade teacher. So, I wrote the petition. The elementary school principal informed me that a letter would be mailed with their decision within two weeks, although his eyes already conveyed approval.

During the first week of summer break, Trevor and I shopped at a Big Lots store while Josh attended a friend's birthday party. While in line at the checkout, I noticed a refrigerated bottled drink cooler three isles away. The advertising trick worked because I suddenly desired an ice-cold drink as the sign indicated. I held my place in line, then asked my tiny five-year-old for help. "Trevor, do you think you can reach the top shelf of that cooler over there to get a coke for me?"

Without moving his feet, Trevor stood next to me, extended his arms in the direction of the drink cooler three isles away, and then announced, "Nope."

The lady behind us giggled at his humor. Amazingly, Trevor didn't seem to be bothered by being overheard unintentionally. Instead, he smiled proudly at his joke. As I moved the hair out of his eyes, I offered him a huge grin. Then, I rephrased my question.

"Ok, smart butt, how about you walk over to the machine—then, will you please try to get the coke for me? It's on the top shelf." He maintained his wide grin the whole way over to the fridge. We both discovered he was tall enough to stretch his little arm to the top shelf and retrieve a coke for his dear old mom.

I was overjoyed when he used his voice in public but worried about bringing attention to him. So, I used the excuse of his physical accomplishment to express my excitement. "That is so awesome, Trevor! I'm so proud of you!"

He didn't respond verbally to my remark, but he didn't cower from being overheard in public either. Today was successful. Trevor used his voice in public. I didn't want to bring attention to his victory directly. So, after we were safely in the car, I phrased his accomplishment with careful consideration. "You have a great sense of humor, Trevor. Even that lady behind us laughed at your joke; that was so funny."

"I just did what you asked," he replied smugly while he held in a giggle.

"Yea, kiddo, sometimes you're just too literal," I responded with a little wink and a wide smile. My eyes shined with glee from the secret behind my excitement.

CHAPTER 11

Saying Hi in First Grade

We received the approval letter a week after summer break began. It felt like a big victory, being granted permission for Trevor to be in Mrs. Powell's class for first grade. Now the new school year was approaching, and there was a buzz of excitement in the air. The boys were elated and chattered often about the upcoming days they would spend with new friends. Josh was especially excited since this was his final year in elementary school. He embraced the unofficial fifth-grade-cool-kid title.

Trevor's anticipation was not shadowed by Josh in any way. His excitement focused on the fact that he would no longer be among the youngest children in the school. He was more mature, moving into a different hall of the school building. No longer being the "little kid" in the school was the confidence booster he needed. But would he find enough courage to break his old habits and use his voice this year? I was hopeful but fearful. I felt helpless and frustrated that I was unable to magically fix his problems. Trevor had to face this on his own. I could only offer my support whether he succeeded or failed.

The first day of our new routine went off without a hitch. The boys scrambled to get ready on time in the morning, eager to ride the bus again with their friends. My foot was already in the door with Trevor's teacher, so volunteer sign-up was a breeze. Josh's fifth grade teacher was new, so he was more than willing to take me on as a helper. The biggest transition for Trevor was that his teacher had remarried over the summer and changed her name. She was no longer Mrs. Powell; she became Mrs. Boyer. This confused more than the children because everyone knew her as *Mrs.* and not *Ms.* or *Miss*, giving the impression she was already married. But she had been divorced prior and felt it was simpler to continue as Mrs. Powell. Plus, it was easier for the children to say. So, Trevor's easy transition into first grade hit a little bump in the road. He didn't seem bothered by it much. At least, he didn't communicate any issues with me about the name change. On the first day of school, he was more focused on the new rule he had to follow, which caused him stress. On the way home in the car, he told me the news.

"Mrs. Boyer said I have to answer her when she calls my name," he stated with a slight quiver in his voice.

"Oh, you mean when she does roll call?" I inquired further.

"Yea. She wants everyone to say, "Hi, Mrs. Boyer," but she told me I can just say hi for now." I glanced in the rearview mirror and was met with worrisome eyes staring back at me.

"So, did you follow her rule?" I asked hesitantly, fearful of his answer.

"Not yet, I have to tomorrow. She said we're bigger now and have to follow the rules as all the first graders do." His voice floated on the brim of emotion and threatened to spill out in the form of tears at any moment.

"Well, it makes sense that she's just trying to get all of her students to follow the rules. Especially since you're older now. First graders are expected to lead the kindergarteners," I offered, hopeful to provide comfort. "Kindergarten was just to get you familiar with school and to learn how to make friends."

Within a few moments the redness around his eyes began to disappear, and his expression changed to acceptance. Trevor nodded his little head as he considered my words. "Yea, I guess you're right. I am a first grader now—that's what Mrs. Boyer said too."

I saw the fear dissolving into determination as I sneaked a peek in the rearview mirror again. That was the moment I knew my child would be able to talk in school, eventually. He was a rule follower and receptive to structure. It helped him to prepare when he knew exactly what to expect. Our eyes locked as we looked into the rearview mirror. I smiled in response and squeezed my eyelids tight in a mimic of a hug to comfort my child.

The next day my nervous stomach returned in response to the fears coursing through my son that morning. He knew what he had to do, but getting his mouth to cooperate might be more challenging than his determination. I did not talk to him about using his voice in class. That would make the fear stronger, give it life.

Instead I got up early and prepared his favorite breakfast. The smell of Toaster Strudels drifted in the air and aroused my boys from their bedroom, coaxing them to the kitchen. Trevor's stoic expression enhanced his pale features. My heart ached in response to the sight of my son. The stress weighed so heavily on his tiny frame. All I could do was distract him with sweetness. As I handed a Toaster Strudel to Trevor, he managed a slight smile of appreciation. Josh was a chatterbox as he gobbled his strudel in only a few bites.

After breakfast we gathered our belongings and moved as a herd out the door and toward the car. Trevor's mood seemed lifted by his brother's enthusiasm. If the presence of worry weren't so heavy, I would have enjoyed the moment with the two boys getting along. They walked side by side like friends to the car. There's a fine line between love and hate. Maybe that phrase originated to describe brothers. If they weren't arguing with one another, they were each other's best friend. Today was the latter, and I prayed it would help Trevor foster the courage he needed to face his fear.

The day dragged on in anticipation of the news only my young son held. Did he tackle his anxiety and manage to force out the single word *hi* in front of his peers? Did he answer his teacher aloud and follow her rule? These questions continued to surface throughout my workday, and I struggled to push them to the back of my mind.

Why did the clock hands seem to slow down when I needed them to speed up?

Finally, school was out for the day. I raced to the bus stop near their dad's house and awaited the arrival of my precious packages. When the bus pulled up, I witnessed two happy, smiling boys descending the bus stairs. So far, so good. Each child received his warm "welcome home" embrace, then made his way to our car. It took all my strength to hold back the big question mulling in my mind about Trevor speaking in class. I did not want to trigger a meltdown. So, I began with a generic "How was your day?" directed at both boys.

"Awesome!" said Josh, eager to share all the details of his day's highlights. Trevor quickly grew tired of hearing about Josh. The moment he climbed into the car, he began his routine and kicked the back of Josh's seat. His tearful screaming joined his flailing feet. Overloaded by stress, Trevor's meltdown was initiated, and Josh became his target.

The boys argued briefly until my intervention. "Stop it, both of you!" I yelled, matching their volume. "Let's listen to some music until we get home. Then, we can talk about anything you need to talk about." Josh wasn't happy that his emotional high was squashed so quickly, but he accepted the routine. With an agreeable nod he turned on the radio and adjusted the volume to drown out the whimpers of his little brother in the back seat. The fifteen-minute drive home felt like an hour.

After the boys ate their snacks, Josh disappeared to his room. He was eager to get onto the computer to play games. Trevor pulled out some paper and began to color, one of his favorite pastimes and stress relievers. Now was the best time to address the elephant in the room. So, I asked, "Hey, sweetie, how was your day at school?"

Without looking away from his artwork, Trevor answered, "It was fine."

"Did you do anything different today?" I attempted to ease into the big question.

"Everything's different. We've only been in school two days," he replied matter-of-factly.

"Did you follow Mrs. Boyer's rule this morning when she called your name?" Finally, the big question was out of the box. I held my breath and awaited his answer.

"Yea, I said hi like she wanted me to," he replied with emotional rawness.

Exhaling my relief, I carefully chose my next words. It was important to follow the doctor's instructions and not make a big deal about Trevor using his voice. So, I simply said, "Good, I'm sure it makes her happy when you follow her rules."

Trevor nodded, then continued coloring. I wanted desperately to hug him, to praise him for his successful first time using his voice in school. But I held back the urge to jump up and down from the bubbling pride and instead leaned over and kissed the top of his head. Then, I followed up with "If you ever need to talk to me about anything, I'm here, and I'll listen."

His precious smile warmed my heart as our eyes made brief contact. No more words were spoken. But the seed of communication was planted.

CHAPTER 12

Selective Mutism Is Much More than Being Silent

The first week of school was only three days long, which flew by. The planned short week was to aid in an easier transition from summer hours to school hours. All of my friends and family were made aware of Trevor's success in using his voice in school. I was overjoyed that he spoke two days in a row. Although I hadn't confirmed with his teacher, I trusted Trevor's story. His stress levels seemed unchanged, however. He still lashed out in anger at the slightest issue. But it hadn't increased either, so I took it as a win!

Finally, my volunteer day arrived. I desperately wanted to discuss Trevor's new verbal status with his teacher. The boys wanted to ride the bus with their friends, so after I dropped them off at the bus stop near their father's house, I raced to the school. Mrs. Boyer was writing today's assignment on the chalkboard as I poked my head into her classroom. The second she finished writing, I knocked on the door frame, alerting her to my presence. She turned to face me, and her smile widened.

"Oh, I was hoping you'd drop in before the kids arrive," Mrs. Boyer announced enthusiastically.

My eyes widened in anticipation of the good news about Trevor using his voice. But I allowed her time to reveal the success.

"He did it! Trevor said hi two days in a row last week and then again two days this week when I called his name," she said excitedly. "I was worried he might have trouble on Monday with the weekend interrupting his routine, but he did fine."

"Oh my gosh, that is such wonderful news!" I answered, full of pride as I clapped my hands together in excitement. "He told me he said hi. Thank you so much for encouraging this huge accomplishment."

"I'm hopeful in the next couple of months he will be able to say the whole "Hi, Mrs. Boyer" response like all the other kids. But for now, his *hi* is acceptable.

"Although, I sort of forced him to do it." She explained matter-of-factly, "I simply explained that he shouldn't be treated any differently than any other child, so he needs to follow the rule for answering just like all the other children."

Our combined excitement at Trevor's accomplishment saying one little word filled the room with positive energy. We both were elated at his success and hopeful this was only the beginning of a spectacular school year.

Neither of us realized how long our joyful chatting lasted and were surprised when the first graders trickled into the classroom. Mrs. Boyer immediately switched to teacher mode. She returned to the front of the room and grabbed some papers from her desk, then assigned me my first task for the day. After I received my instructions on what to do with the stack of papers, I started toward the door. Trevor turned the corner in the hall and headed toward the room as I exited the doorway. I offered a little wink and a subtle "I love you" sign from under the stack of papers in my arms. My gesture was noticed. His little smile and quick flash of "I love you" with his tiny hand warmed my heart. No one else was privy to our bonding moment. The emotional high carried me down the hall to the office copy machine.

A few months passed without any new improvements with Trevor's public speaking. He still only managed the single word, *hi*, when called upon in class. But Mrs. Boyer noticed he was more involved physically with the other kids. Once he even raised his hand when she asked for a volunteer to help collect the erasers for cleaning. Granted, there were no voice skills necessary for this task, but it was a huge step in combating his social anxiety. He had allowed himself to be singled out as a volunteer.

Trevor's recollection of the event was slightly different from his teacher's view. He told me his friend Austin talked him into cleaning erasers with him at school, and he simply went along with it. That didn't lessen my elation of his accomplishment. He still held his hand high enough to be seen by everyone when the teacher asked for volunteers. He stood out in the crowd and brought attention to himself. That was a hugely successful moment, and pride swelled inside of me. I wanted to burst out in song. I knew my son would be upset if I made a big deal out of his accomplishment, so I opted for a smile and casual "sounds fun" comment instead. His smile assured me I had chosen correctly.

Winter break approached, and Mrs. Boyer mentioned how Trevor still had not lengthened his response during attendance. "After we return from break, I expect Trevor to answer with the full sentence as all the other children do in class. He has had enough time to prepare for this change," she stated.

I knew she wasn't wrong, and I longed for Trevor to be like all the other children using their voices. But my stomach dived in response to her statement. How could I help my child accomplish this task? Months had passed, and he wasn't any closer to speaking in school. My forced smile did not reach my eyes as I agreed with his teacher. "I will talk to him about it over break and make sure he follows your rules."

"Great. I know he can do it if he puts his mind to it," she continued, her reassurance softening the harshness of her demand.

The boys were excited about having two weeks off school. I had purchased snowshoes on clearance last spring, hopeful they would get a chance to use them this winter. But we lived in Ohio, which has unpredictable weather. Sometimes it would snow heavily in December, but usually we had little snowfall until January or February. Josh and Trevor were hopeful this winter break would be white so they could walk on top of the snow in their new snowshoes. Unfortunately, this winter break was green and dry. There was no sledding or snowboarding and no walking on top of snow for either of them. Their new snowshoes remained tucked away along with my hopes for an energetic activity to fill their empty days.

It was challenging to find entertaining projects to capture the boys' attention when they were stuck inside the house for long periods. The temperature was too cold outside to play. Without snow, outdoor activities would not be fun anyway. The most recent subscription of *Family Fun* magazine arrived and offered a few creative ideas for passing time. Unfortunately, my young, energetic boys did not share my enthusiasm for the paper crafts. I found myself doing the crafts alone while they played video games on their Nintendo gaming system. Admittedly, the sounds of joyful cheering that filled the air made me happier than any shared craft project as I embraced the moments the boys played happily together. But this calm always came before the storm. It was only a matter of time until someone would break the playful banter.

The first to scream was Trevor as I would have expected. Being younger, he struggled with the video games, which were often geared toward older children. Josh replied with nearly equal volume. He yelled something about Trevor and a broken controller. My guess was Trevor threw the game controller in his brother's direction. Not *at* his brother—that would be too obvious. No, he probably threw it close enough to alert Josh of his anger, possibly hopeful that it would bounce and hit him. Indirect hitting is only an accident, right? It was time to intervene before more than the controller got broken. I

61

left my cute little teddy bear craft project half finished on the table and walked into the family room, ready to bare my teeth. But Trevor pushed past me and stomped his feet down the hall toward his room. Josh and I stared in the direction of the bedroom. With half-closed eyelids, we anticipated the door slam we were about to hear. *Bam!* The walls jarred in response to his angry outburst.

"Why does he do those things?" Josh asked as he investigated the broken controller.

"He's a lot younger than you, sweetie. These games are harder for him. He gets frustrated and lashes out," I explained.

"I get frustrated, too, and I don't throw controllers. He should know better. I don't like playing with him because he always does this and makes me mad."

I understood why Josh was upset, but I felt torn about how to get through to Trevor. "Josh, I promised I would try to help Trevor find better ways of controlling his anger. I picked up a couple of books at the library on anger management, so maybe now is as good a time as any to work with him on some of the strategies in the books." On that note I turned and headed down the hallway toward my challenge for the day.

First, I stuck my ear against Trevor's door and listened. It was quiet. So, I knocked lightly, then waited. I bit my lower lip in fear of the potential angry response from the other side of the door.

"Who is it!" Trevor questioned harshly.

"It's me, babe. Can I come in?" I spoke as sweetly as I could muster.

"Yea, but *not* Josh, he can't come in!" Trevor announced with conviction.

I pushed the door open enough to squeeze through, then entered the lion's den. One deep breath prepared me to speak gently to my angry child.

"Sweetie, I read this book that gave some ideas on how to calm down when angry. I'd like to try them with you."

He glared in my direction as he analyzed my body language. Then, he replied, "What are they?"

Relief flowed through me; the lion was letting me remove his thorn. Remaining tactful, I discussed the anger management techniques listed in the book. "One really good technique said to tighten each muscle group. Start at your feet—wiggle your toes, pump your ankles, raise your legs—and then work your way up to your head. After one cycle, take a deep breath and reverse the order. This helps the anger to flow out of your body and gives you a feeling of calmness," I stated with persuasion. "Here, let's try it together."

We completed two cycles of the stress relief method. "Thanks, I do feel a little better," Trevor stated in a much calmer voice. After I embraced him in a hug, Trevor opened the flood gates, venting his frustrations. "Josh is so mean to me. He says things on purpose to make me mad. Why is he always so mean?" The emotion in his voice threatened to spill over into tears at any moment.

"Sweetie, your brother gets frustrated too. I don't think he's trying to push your buttons and make you mad," I reassured.

"Yes, he is! He knows exactly what he's doing," Trevor replied, still on the brink of tears.

"Maybe you shouldn't play video games with him. After all, those games are made for bigger kids."

Trevor's sad expression broke my heart. Then, he admitted, "I like playing with Josh. He's my brother, and I want him to like me too. But I don't think he likes me." He no longer held back the tears after this admission, and soon his pink cheeks glistened with streaks of silver-white.

I hugged him tightly and rocked back and forth, hopeful to squeeze the sadness out of my baby. Deep down he simply wanted to feel loved like any human being. And even though I knew his brother did love him, I also knew he could be difficult to deal with at times. Especially times like these when his anxieties were high.

As an adult I sometimes struggled to handle Trevor's outbursts and lacked the necessary patience. His ten-year-old brother hadn't learned the life skills necessary to deal with challenging people. So, of course, he got more frustrated with his younger brother. At that moment there were no right words to ease my baby's pain. So, I sat there and held him until his little sobs eventually lessened. Selective mutism is much more than being silent.

CHAPTER 13

Breakthrough Blessings

Preparing Trevor to speak a sentence in class was a daunting task. If I mentioned it too often, he would get upset and shutdown. But I feared if I didn't mention it at all, he might not be able to say the words his teacher required. I approached Trevor while he used the paint program on the computer. He was happiest creating works of abstract art.

"Remember, Mrs. Boyer wants you to be like all the other kids when she calls your name on Monday morning. Do you know how you're supposed to answer?"

"Yea, I know. 'Hi, Mrs. Boyer.'" He replied without moving his gaze from the monitor.

"That's perfect. She'll be happy you're following her rules." I announced, feeling hopeful, then watched as he added royal blue into the random design on the screen. A vibrant abstract artwork was coming to life before my eyes. He mixed in small dabs of yellow, then filled the background with grayish purple.

I prepared Trevor for the future by offering possible outcomes. This was the best approach to overcoming his anxiety from selective mutism. If he knew what was expected and had an idea of the possible scenarios, he had more courage to face the task at hand. So, I painted a picture figuratively as Trevor literally painted his. He added a deep red-orange into the mix.

"Monday, when Mrs. Boyer calls your name and you say, 'Hi, Mrs. Boyer,' some of the other kids might overhear your conversation with the teacher," I said delicately.

Was that an eye roll from my five-year-old son? "Uh, yea, everyone hears when she calls our names," He announced, as if my "might overhear" comment was the stupidest thing he had ever heard.

I smiled warmly in response, then continued. "Yes, I suppose you are right. Anyway, the kids have already heard your usual answer of saying hi, but they might notice you're finally following the teacher's instructions and saying her name too. They might say something to you about it." To reassure him, I then said, "You should be prepared if they bring it to your attention. Maybe you can just smile at them or ignore them, whatever you choose."

After a brief pause he nodded, then returned to his computer. He closed the paint program and reached for one of his CDs—*Adiboo: Magical Playland*. After he inserted it into the CD-ROM, he waited for the screen to begin his new adventure. I interpreted this redirection of focus as the end of our conversation. I hoped my pep talk worked to help him overcome the anxiety of using his voice in class.

Monday morning came around quickly. The boys were eager to see their friends at school after being apart for two weeks. Hope remained in my thoughts as I imagined Trevor answering his teacher with the full sentence she required. I believed he could do it, but doubtful fear remained. My workday passed slowly, but finally it came time to meet the boys at the bus stop.

Trevor descended the bus steps first and ran up to me. Surprisingly, he announced, "I did it, I said the whole thing to Mrs. Boyer."

Stunned by his openness, I replied without thought. "Really? You used your voice and said the whole sentence?" Fear raced through my mind as I made a direct acknowledgment of his public talking. Would he shut down? Would he get angry? But he seemed emotionally stronger today, although I knew his anxiety could be triggered at any time. His eyes widened, and then Josh came bounding up before he could respond.

"Trevor, did you hear about the cat that got into the school today?" Josh asked excitedly.

Turning abruptly to Josh, Trevor's attention was averted away from our conversation, and he immediately engaged with his brother. "I heard about that, but I didn't see it. How'd it happen?" Trevor's excitement matched Josh's, and the two chatted about the furry friend entering the building behind some kids returning from recess.

My panic eased as I listened to the brothers conversing. Why couldn't they get along like this all the time? We made it home without any arguments or seat-kicking. I was overjoyed that Trevor managed to talk aloud in class and relieved he didn't have a meltdown in the car. Today was a total success. This called for a celebration. My soon-to-be husband, Nick suggested we go out to eat in recognition of the fantastic day. I mentioned this idea to the boys, and they were eager to eat out. Both agreed on Fazoli's restaurant. I knew Trevor didn't like red sauce, so this choice concerned me. He loved the garlic butter breadsticks, which were replenished at our table every time we ate there, but breadsticks are not a balanced meal. I suggested Trevor order the pizza. Instead, he chose spaghetti without sauce. The restaurant didn't offer an alternative topping for the spaghetti, so he received a plate full of naked noodles. No surprise when he didn't eat much off his plate. But he managed to put away four breadsticks on his own. With his picky food preferences, I worried about Trevor's health. The multivitamin gummy he was taking sure had its work cut out for it.

Later that evening I felt compelled to discuss today's accomplishment with Trevor. This time I vowed not to explicitly mention his public speaking. If it hadn't been for his brother's distraction earlier in the day, I'm unsure how my comment might have affected him. Fear still guided my emotions, and I wondered if my baby had been traumatized.

"Hey, sweetie, I just wanted to tell you again how proud I am that you followed the rules in school today. I'm sure Mrs. Boyer was pleased too." I omitted the speech portion to make it less direct.

"I said I would do it. Didn't you believe me?" Trevor asked questioningly.

"Of course, I never doubted you for a moment," I replied as I attempted a convincing smile. "But sometimes things happen that are out of our control and interfere with our plans. Even if we're strong, things happen. So, I'm glad nothing happened to prevent you from accomplishing your goal today." I realized my nervous rambling was probably not making much sense, so I tried to drop the subject.

"What things can happen?" He inquired, not letting me drop the subject so easily.

"Oh, I don't know. Maybe we think we can do something, then when we try, we discover it's harder than we thought. Like if I tell myself I can get close to a spider. It's easier to imagine I can do it when there's no spider around. But as soon as a spider crawls close to me, I discover I can't control my fear; I have to run away from the scary creature."

Trevor widened his eyes and giggled at me. "Yea, I can imagine you running away from a tiny spider."

"See, babe? We're all afraid of something. Everyone. Even if people say they're not afraid, secretly they are. Fear is a part of being human. I'm sure there's stuff you're afraid of too," I said.

"Yea, I'm afraid of talking in school," he admitted as he diverted his eyes away from mine and focused on the floor, the rawness from his emotion apparent in his voice.

"Are you worried the other kids will make fun of you?" I asked, worried he may shut down at any moment from my prying.

"No. Well, maybe. I don't know, it's just hard. It's like I want to talk to my friends, but I just can't." Trevor's honesty surprised me. I had longed for this conversation, and it felt like a huge breakthrough. But I knew the importance of going at his pace.

"I'm sure it'll get easier as time goes by. And next year will be even easier because you'll have a classroom full of new people, kids who don't even know you yet," I added. "Kids who never even knew you didn't talk in class when you were younger."

Trevor nodded and hugged me quickly, then walked away toward his bedroom. It didn't take a sign language expert to read his body language—he was finished with this conversation. I sat there for a moment and smiled while I thought about all the day's successes. Then, I raced to the family room and shared my joy in hushed whispers to Nick.

CHAPTER 14

A Shred of Normalcy

February approached, which meant my baby would be turning seven. Our family always celebrated the kids' birthdays with a huge party and cake. Every party was themed, which helped coax guests into attending. Although, Trevor never seemed to have any issues with gaining friends. This confused me. How could he have friends if he never talked to them? Maybe boys were different from girls? Or maybe he somehow managed to communicate with his friends nonverbally? Whatever the circumstances, he enjoyed school and the kids in his class. Trevor was the only silent yet outgoing person I had ever met. Initially it confused me that he had selective mutism even though he was not shy or introverted. But I learned that SM is not a personality trait.

For Trevor's seventh birthday party we decided on a bowling theme. It seemed the perfect way to bring in the lucky number milestone. Traditionally we made handmade invitations, which offered a personal touch. Trevor's teacher required invitations to be given to every student in the class so no one was left out. So, we diligently created twenty bowling pin-shaped invitations for this year's party.

The end of February arrived quickly. The morning of Trevor's birthday I made pancakes for breakfast. My attempted pancake shape of Mickey Mouse failed miserably. The pancakes appeared more as three blobs combining into a deformed heart. But Trevor didn't mind—he ate them appreciatively. Fridays were always filled with excitement, being the end of the week. But having a birthday on a Friday made it even better. Even Josh was happy, having reaped Trevor's reward of the pancake breakfast. I dropped the boys off outside the school and exchanged our "I love you" signs. My car remained parked until they disappeared into the building.

I got off early enough from work to make a detour to the party supply store. After I purchased a poster board, markers, and seven balloons, each with the number seven on them, I began my plan. I sat in the car and drew out a sign that read "HAPPY 7th BIRTHDAY, TREVOR!" I arrived at the school just a few minutes before release and awaited the dismissal bell. The office lady spotted me through the window and smiled widely at the sight. Nearly the moment the bell rang, the kids trickled out of the adjacent hallways. Many students asked for a balloon, but most simply smiled and waved. I stood tall and awaited the first graders to approach. Silently I prayed my child would love this attention. It could go badly, but I hadn't considered the possibility until that very moment. Panic suddenly struck me. What if he was so embarrassed by my gesture that it caused him to revert to not talking at all? Fortunately, I didn't have long to deliberate on this negativity because I spotted Trevor among the mass of young faces moving in my direction. His huge smile and bright eyes conveyed approval of my action. Trevor's friends patted him on the back and pointed at the sign as they neared. One mumbled something about "You're so lucky." Another said, "See you tonight at your party." Both friends wished him a happy birthday and went out the door toward their corresponding buses. Trevor joined me, and then we went out the door toward the parking lot. I think he grew a full inch since morning because he walked taller than I remembered. Happiness flowed through me and warmed my core. I made my child feel special like he deserved. And I felt confident that at least one friend was coming to his party. We both bounced to the car with a little skip in our step, eager for the evening's festivities.

Six of the twenty invited children showed up to Trevor's party that evening. Overall, I considered thirty percent acceptance as successful attendance. There were even two girls who attended, which added a little fun to the dynamics of the event. We rented two bowling lanes and the party room, where they enjoyed pizza and cake. While Trevor was excited about the celebration, his tight-jawed, serious expression also gave hint to the anxiety he struggled to control. Theoretically he loved the attention. But having selective mutism, he also dreaded it. He spent the entire evening silent with an occasional smile or nod. His friends didn't seem to notice anything unusual with Trevor's personality; obviously this was his normal behavior around them. One of the girls asked me if Trevor ever talked at home. Her curiosity was piqued when I answered yes, all the time. Although his classmates realized he knew how to speak because he answered their teacher in the mornings, he had never verbalized more than a few words, which led them to believe he was mostly mute. I tried to be inconspicuous and explain Trevor's issue to the kids without Trevor overhearing. Only the girls were close enough to hear my explanation. There seemed to be an invisible glue that held the boys together because their pack didn't separate the whole evening. These were the classmates Trevor always talked about—these were his friends. As I watched them talk to Trevor, I saw them pat his back fondly. And they laughed together, which created mixed emotions. I should have felt happy, pleased he was interacting in some form. Instead I felt sad. It pained me to see him holding back, not being fully engaged in their comradery. I longed for my baby to be normal.

As the festivities wound down, we all gathered in the party room around the gift table. There were colorful paper-wrapped boxes and fun printed bags. The boys pushed their way to the front, as close to Trevor as possible. Each friend wanted him to open their gift first. Hearing a knock at the door distracted everyone for a moment. In walked an employee of the bowling alley carrying a bowling pin. He asked, "Which one is the birthday boy?" Trevor remained silent as his friends all pointed in his direction indicating the answer. The young man held out the pin, then announced it was his to keep as a memento of this special occasion. Trevor managed a small smile but avoided eye contact with the worker. As he reached for the pin, he hadn't expected it to be so heavy. Trevor nearly dropped it onto the floor the moment the exchange happened. But he tightened his arms around it just in time, and his friends cheered at the averted catastrophe. The worker handed me a black permanent marker and suggested each attendee sign the pin. The children were interested and wanted to touch the big, white, hourglass-shaped object. They ogled the smooth surface. Of course, they each wanted to hold it themselves and feel the weight of a real bowling pin. One of the boys bragged it wasn't that heavy right before it nearly slipped through his hands. A few giggles later they each had a turn at signing the object of interest. Trevor appeared to be more relaxed and laughed aloud at the silliness of his friends.

After the bowling pin fun, Trevor's friends returned their focus to his presents. One said, "Open mine first," while another wanted his opened first. The battle for gift order symbolized their friendship ranking. As Trevor's mother, I trumped all others. So, I announced he would be opening his parents' gift first. I handed Trevor the small, rectangular package, and the boys began a guessing game as to the contents.

"I bet it's a book," one exclaimed.

"I think it's a game," another guessed.

"No, it looks more like a DVD," a third friend declared.

Trevor tore off the paper slowly. His huge smile reached his eyes with a brief sparkle of excitement. It was the DVD movie he had wanted: *Bionicle: Mask of Light—The Movie*. Suddenly Trevor realized he was displaying emotion for all to see. Nearly immediately he dropped his smile, and his eyes widened in fear. His friends didn't seem to notice. They were too preoccupied with his gifts being revealed and shoved another into his hands. I watched as Trevor opened each package: a Lego Bionicle, an Air Hog airplane—even an Operation game was among his prizes. He offered a slight smile but fought the urge to indulge more. It pained me to watch as my son appeared to be unappreciative of his presents. I knew he loved having received the gifts and greatly appreciated their gestures. But the spotlight became more than he could handle. I decided he'd had enough stimulation for one night and thanked each child for the wonderful gifts. Fortunately, it was time for their parents to pick them up. We sent a goodie bag with each child as a token of our appreciation for their support of Trevor.

On the ride home Trevor began a meltdown. He focused his anger at Josh and yelled, "Leave me alone. Stop looking at me!" His brother responded with equal volume and anger. A screaming war began in our back seat. We were trapped inside the small box together with screeching little boy voices, which echoed off the windows. I glanced at Nick for guidance, but he was as baffled as I on how to handle this situation. All I could think to do was redirect Trevor's attention, so I asked him which was the favorite toy he received from his friends. Amazingly, it worked, at least for the remaining few minutes' drive to our destination.

We arrived home before another angry outburst. Trevor gathered his favorite toys and ran for the house. All in all, it was an exhaustingly fun and successful day. And for brief moments during the party, Trevor was simply another seven-year-old. Normalcy was the best gift that night, even if it only came in small bursts through smiles or laughter. Moments like those led me to believe there was a bright future for my baby, a normal life ahead. Hope remained.

CHAPTER 15

Left Out

Trevor enjoyed art and eagerly helped create the birthday thank-you notes. He was less enthusiastic about passing them out to his friends. I knew his anxiety would be piqued, so I informed his teacher ahead of time. Mrs. Boyer was quite attentive to the children's needs and easily accepted the request to nudge him in the right direction. His silent birthday appreciation was expressed in written form. Trevor managed to thank each one of his attendees in his own special way. It seemed odd how he could write but not speak to the other children. If we had had cell phones readily available like in today's modern world, I am sure he would have used texting as his form of communication. But we survived with paper communication, and Trevor's thank-you cards were his first correspondence with his friends. I am sure many thought I made the cards alone. But I was the mere helper who kept his secret voice safe.

Spring approached—it was time to sign the boys up for baseball. Last year Trevor played ragball, which is a form of T-ball for younger children but played with a softer ball. This year his age group advanced him into T-ball. Trevor enjoyed group sports, and he easily joined into the silent physical activity. His coaches appreciated Trevor's quietness, which gave them the impression he was a great listener. They did not realize his anxiety prevented him from conversing with his teammates. Although I educated each coach about selective mutism and requested they not treat him differently than the other kids, they still did not fully comprehend his issue and had never heard of selective mutism before our encounter. In fact, throughout our journey no one had heard of the disorder before we came along. I did my best to spread the knowledge about the anxiety issue and happily answered their questions. Even though little was known publicly about SM, having lived with a child suffering from the diagnosis automatically made us experts in the area.

T-ball picture day came quickly. Before the first game the kids lined up in front of the four coaches in two rows on the ball field. Trevor was in the back row on the far right—the far, far right. He was so far out to the right, away from the other boys, that the photographer asked him to move in. "You on the end, move in a bit, just a little more . . . a little more . . . one more step . . ." Finally, he gave up and snapped the photo, which displayed our son at least a foot away from the group. Trevor wore a smile, so we considered it a win that day.

Tackling anxiety is not easily accomplished, but Trevor made baby steps every day. His body language was louder than his voice at this point in his progress. Each small improvement got him closer to learning how to overcome this horrendous obstacle. After I realized his chosen placement for this photo, I investigated his previous sports photos for comparison. Trevor played ragball the previous year and had finished two seasons of soccer. Out of the three previous team sports photos, all showed my apprehensive son standing off to the side of the group. And he consistently wore a slightly forced smile. How had I not noticed this before? Every year he intentionally placed himself off to the edge, as far as possible from the other kids. He followed some unknown rule that he belonged on the outskirts. As I pondered the photos, it made sense. Social groups require confidence, something my child lacked because of the selective mutism. I longed for the day I would see Trevor's smiling face in the middle of the pack and wondered if that dream would ever come to life.

The end of the school year neared without Trevor having found his voice with his friends. I feared this was his permanent, established routine and searched for a way to break his pattern. I started by asking the second grade teachers if anyone had experience with selective mutism. Out of the two teachers, one knew about the anxiety. She said she taught a little girl many years prior who suffered from it. Hope rose to the surface of my emotions. I asked her if the girl ever learned to speak publicly. She replied, "Unfortunately, her family moved only a couple of months into the school year, so I didn't have enough time to develop enough trust with her to bring her out of her shell." But she reassured me, saying, "She did begin to engage with the other children more and showed signs of progression before leaving the school."

The kind-eyed teacher smiled with compassion. I knew right away: she was the teacher Trevor needed. I trusted Mrs. Reno. So, I petitioned for a specific teacher placement again. By now I was used to the whole process and marched right into the principal's office with my request. I'm not sure if it was my whole page written explanation as to why my child needed to be in Mrs. Reno's class or if it was my history volunteering weekly at the school that got the approval through so fast. Whatever the reason, I appreciated it. Trevor had a fighting chance to be normal next school year. I was determined to do everything within my power to help him break through this invisible wall of silence.

I received the dreaded call from Julie, the boys' summer babysitter. She had decided to take on a full-time job away from the home this summer. Unsure what to do with the boys while I worked, I feared a problematic three-month future before second grade began. Having found Julie was a blessing for us. She helped Trevor feel comfortable and allowed him to be himself while in her home. How could we ever find another babysitter as gentle-natured and understanding as Julie? Panic rose within me the second I heard the news, but I fought to push it back down quickly after hanging up the phone. We did it once, and we could do it again—or at least, I hoped.

I interviewed babysitters, which caused my stressful fears to grow. No one had heard of or understood selective mutism. Many thought Trevor should be forced into speaking. I refused to allow that to happen. After the third failed interview, a neighbor stepped forward. "I'm home during the mornings and afternoons before work, so I could watch your boys for a few days until you find someone," Pam politely offered.

I was ecstatic at her suggestion and felt confident Trevor would be comfortable in her home. He was already acquainted with her son.

"Yes, that would be wonderful, Pam. Thank you so much!" I couldn't contain my excitement and rambled on. "I'm sure Trevor will be so happy to be close to home. And he already knows you and your son. This will be perfect, thank you!"

Pam misunderstood my enthusiasm and misheard it as "Thank you for offering to watch my boys forever." She immediately responded to clarify her offer. "Just for a few days until you can find a permanent babysitter."

Her shoulders dropped in relief when I reassured her I had understood the temporary condition of her offer, although secretly I hoped she would change her mind after she realized how easy it would be to watch the boys. I imagined she would be begging me to allow a long-term commitment. After we worked out a fair price, I felt happy and encouraged, ready for summer break.

The last two weeks of school were busy with final exams, school assemblies, and a special event called Field Day. Every year I attended Field Day and watched the kids let loose outside in the big affair of games and fun. This year they had a huge red blow-up ball, which each team pushed from one orange coned area to another in a timed event. The wind joined in on the game and blew the ball out of boundaries several times when Trevor's team was up. With a slower time, they did not win first place, but their giggles won special memories in their hearts and mine.

Josh was also exceptionally excited, having won one of five top athletic awards presented by the gym teacher during an assembly. By the huge smile on Trevor's face, I knew he also was proud of his big brother. But a hint of worry remained behind his eyes. This was the last year they would ever be in the same building throughout their entire remaining school days. I understood his fear. Change is hard, especially for Trevor, who thrived on routine. But my child was strong. He could tackle anything if he was prepared. And that was exactly what I planned on helping him do: prepare for the summer and prepare for second grade.

CHAPTER 16

Babysitter Blues

I appreciated the convenience of walking a few houses down the street for babysitting services. Our previous sitter lived across the city, which made the trek much longer. Pam was awake and ready to receive the boys that first babysitting morning. She even had her full makeup applied with her normal orangey-toned foundation. She reminded me of a blonde Oompa Loompa from *Charlie and the Chocolate Factory*, only taller. Her friendly smile helped redirect attention to her personality rather than her ill-matching foundation choice.

"Hi, Trevor," Pam announced as she embraced the opportunity to help my problem child.

No reply was uttered from Trevor's mouth. He glanced away, searching for anything to divert his attention. I recognized the fear in his body language right away, but it made no sense. He knew Pam. He's been in this house several times and played with her son. Why would he react so differently this morning? While I pondered this thought, Pam continued to speak as if nothing was wrong.

"I have some snacks ready whenever you get hungry. I wasn't sure what you'd want for lunch, but I can make mac 'n' cheese or peanut butter and jelly, your choice," she offered sweetly.

Her question remained unanswered as my child stood motionless. My anxiety rose, so I quickly spoke for him. "What kind of mac 'n' cheese do you have? Trevor is a little particular and only likes Velveeta macaroni and cheese from the squeeze packets, not the dry powder mix."

"Oh, I only have the microwave containers. Makes it easier since I don't like to cook," Pam responded candidly.

I glanced in Trevor's direction, and from his blanched complexion and worried look, I knew immediately his take on the food offerings. "I think peanut butter and jelly would be the best choice if you don't mind. Trevor is quite picky when it comes to his mac 'n' cheese, and I wouldn't want the food to be wasted. But thank you so much, Pam, for giving him choices." I hoped my smile and appreciation masked my growing fear.

As we stood near the front door and finalized the details of the day, I turned to hug my child goodbye. Josh had already headed for the backyard, unaffected by my impending departure. Trevor's pale face and wide eyes looked up at me with worry. Confused by his nervous behavior, I reassured him it would be fine. I reminded him about the previous days he had fun when he played at this house. After I leaned down to my child's level, I gave him a comforting hug. Trevor clung to me like a baby monkey and grasped anywhere he could get a hold. I glanced up at Pam and saw her startled expression. We both were confused about this unexpected bout of separation anxiety. Each time I pulled one of his arms off of me, his other arm grasped tightly around my leg or midsection. It was as if my child had octopus tentacles and stuck to anything he touched. "Trevor, what's going on?" I finally asked in desperation.

Tears gathered in his eyes, and he quickly glanced in Pam's direction, then back at me. He remained silent. I bent down farther so my ear was near his mouth. Using my body, I blocked Pam's view and offered Trevor privacy. He finally whispered his concerns. "I don't want you to go, stay here with me."

"Sweetie, I have to go to work. I'll be back in four hours. That's not very long. Just go outside with the other boys and play. I'll be back before you know it."

"No, please, no," he pleaded again in whispers.

"Trevor, are you afraid of Pam?" I asked as I mimicked his hushed tone.

"No, I just don't want you to go."

I told Pam, "Sometimes it's easier to just pull off that bandage. I'm sure he'll be fine as soon as I'm gone." I kissed Trevor's head and peeled his limbs from the death grip he had on me. Then out the door I went.

Just under four hours later I returned to Pam's to pick up the boys. I hoped that Trevor came around and began to have fun soon after I left. But that hope was extinguished the moment I stepped through the door. There he sat next to the front door in the same place I left him. His cheeks glistened with dried tears.

"Oh, I'm so glad you're here," Pam announced in desperation. "Trevor never moved from that same position all day. It just breaks my heart to see him so unhappy here."

I wanted to reassure her. I wanted to explain it was merely his anxieties. But my brain didn't cooperate. I stood there dumbfounded, and my thoughts raced as I tried to make sense of the whole scene. How could a seven-year-old child stay in one position for four hours? As I struggled to grasp this concept, I mumbled my attempted consolation. "Pam, I'm sure it isn't you. Trevor is . . . Trevor is . . . different."

Pam was not reassured. She continued to express her frustrations and sadness that the incident happened. Then, she made a statement that pulled me out of my shock. "I can't do this again. You're going to have to find someone else to watch him."

No! This can't be happening! Who else could I get on such short notice? I took a deep breath and attempted to collect my thoughts. Then I pleaded, "Oh, Pam, I'm sure it won't happen again. I'll talk to him. It isn't you or your home. It has to be something else bothering him."

But Pam wasn't negotiating. "I've never seen a child act like that—there has to be something wrong with him. But I can't go through it again. It was heartbreaking to see him so upset, and there was nothing I could do to fix it."

Confusion still hung in the air, but Pam's words also filtered into my mind. *There must be something wrong with him.* Of course there was something wrong with him—anxiety, that's what was wrong. Pam was in no mood to hear anything I had to say. I got the feeling she wanted us out of her house as fast as humanly possible, that she hoped to erase the horrible experience from her mind by eliminating the visual source. So, I obliged and called for Josh, who was playing downstairs. After I paid Pam for her services, we left her home, never to return.

I frantically rescheduled my work and managed to arrange coverage for the next two days. We needed a reliable, trustworthy babysitter ASAP. But I also wanted to figure out what triggered Trevor to be so stubborn and resistant that he stood at the front door for four hours and refused to eat. Pam said he stood there until his legs became so tired he finally slid down into the sitting position. But as soon as his muscles regained strength, he stood up again. I imagined being on an episode of *Survivor* with the challenge being "to stand in place as long as possible." I doubted I could last more than an hour, even when faced with the possibility of winning money. My child may have won the million dollars if he was on the game show, but unfortunately, this was real life. The only thing we won for his determination was the task of finding a new babysitter.

I discussed our lack-of-babysitter predicament with friends and family. Many suggested perusing the paper for someone or placing an ad. Since this was prior to the smartphone era, the newspaper was our best source for job-hunting services. I scanned the classified section of our city paper for babysitting service offers. Of the four listed, none were in our neck of the woods. A half-hour drive for babysitting services seemed last resort to me, so I opted to search for references in person. Our local grocery store and post office offered a corkboard for people to hang classified ad posters. I found a babysitting name and number on one display that simply read, "I will watch your children in my home 8 AM – 5 PM." After I tore off one of the tabs listing the phone number, I headed for home to make the call.

A pleasant female voice answered. I wanted to like this lady—I *needed* to like this lady. Hopeful she could solve our long-term babysitting issues, I grasped at every positive in our interaction. After we arranged a meeting time at her home, I hung up the phone. If it went well, she agreed to begin immediately watching the boys. The next day couldn't come soon enough as I anticipated meeting the new babysitting prospect.

Josh and Trevor were prepared for the new experience. I pleaded with Trevor beforehand on the importance of having someone watch them for only a few hours. He understood my struggle and reassured me he would try harder to make this work. It's amazing how much more cooperative a child can be when you put it into terms they can grasp. I simply stated that if I cannot work, there will be no money for toys or computer games. In desperation I even threatened that there would be no more buying gummy snacks or eating out at McDonald's. It's not my proudest moment, and I wouldn't win a mother-of-the-year award for my childish retort, but my patience was running thin.

The moment we pulled up in front of Theresa's home, I spotted two boys playing with a soccer ball in the front yard. Josh immediately yelled out from the back seat, "Hey, I know that kid! That's Justin." Opening the door mere moments before we stopped (which reminded me, I needed to switch the child lock back to the *on* setting), he sprinted over to the boys and immediately began chatting with his friends.

Trevor and I climbed out of the car together and headed for the front door. Before we reached it, a slender, dark-haired woman stepped out. She wore a genuine smile, and I immediately liked her.

"I see your son knows my son," Theresa noted.

"Yes, that makes it easier, doesn't it?" I said. "You don't happen to have a seven-year-old, too, do you?" I asked, hopeful for a comparable playmate for Trevor.

"No, sorry. Only the one son and the neighbor boy, but he's ten. Justin has a ton of toys inside that Trevor is welcome to play with if he'd like," Theresa offered.

The three of us walked inside, and Theresa showed Trevor the living room where the toy chest was located. He perused the toy options with growing interest. As he reached deep into the chest, he pulled out a Power Ranger-looking figure. Excitedly he began moving all the parts around and readjusted the armor. My Power Ranger knowledge was limited, but it appeared Trevor knew exactly what he was doing with the toy. And the best part, he looked like he enjoyed it. I wondered if Justin had a room full of Power Rangers to help entertain Trevor for at least four hours.

Theresa then suggested that when he was finished with the toys, he could watch a VHS or DVD movie. She proceeded to list a few titles in their vast collection—*Finding Nemo*, *Holes*, *Cat in the Hat*, and *Spy Kids* were among the few she rattled off. Trevor glanced up, and his eyes glistened with interest in her proposition. I knew he would be fine here for today with all the movie choices. I counted my lucky stars and decided this would be the perfect time to exit while Trevor was preoccupied. So, I briefly discussed today's trial babysitting and gave Theresa multiple methods for reaching me. After I planted a kiss on top of Trevor's head, I walked out the door. A wave goodbye was all Josh needed, but I threw in an "I love you" sign while he watched me leave. For some strange reason it embarrassed my elder son whenever I displayed that sign in public. Josh glanced nervously between the two boys surrounding him and attempted to determine if they comprehended the interaction. When he realized they had not, he offered a proud smile and a quick return of the ASL sign. Hope soared within me as I pulled away and began my workday.

Day one went well with the new sitter, and I couldn't have been happier. Trevor seemed to enjoy his alone time when he played with toys and watched movies. The older boys played outside most of the day, but they did come in for lunch and snacks. Maybe the reduced interaction with other children helped Trevor cope with his anxiety. Or maybe he simply understood how important it was for me to work and earn money to buy him toys. Either way, Theresa was a blessing.

Day two arrived, and both boys seemed eager to go to Theresa's. Trevor talked about which movies he wanted to watch that day, but I worried about what he would do when he ran out of interesting titles. Hopefully by then he would have grown accustomed to his new routine at her home. It was a breeze when I dropped the boys off at the new babysitter that morning. I wondered if this was what parents of normal kids felt like every day. Suddenly, I was jealous of those hypothetical parents. Not that I would trade my boys for anything in the world, but to have this carefree departure every day of life would be satisfyingly peaceful. I shook my head at the thought and decided to appreciate the moment. After we shared kisses and "I love you" ASL signs, I ventured into the world to turn my medical service into money.

The dreaded call came midway through my day. My heart sank the moment Theresa's name appeared on my phone. My mind began racing through all the possibilities that involved Trevor and his anxieties. What had he done now? I finally decided it was best to answer the call and find out what was wrong.

"Um, hello," was my fearful greeting.

"Hi, this is Theresa. We've had an emergency, and I think you need to come right away. I'm so sorry. Josh was playing, and I think he broke his arm."

As I deciphered Theresa's words, it suddenly struck me that she had said *Josh*. What? Had I heard her wrong? Something happened with Josh. That made no sense—she must have meant Trevor. So, I questioned what I heard. "Josh? You mean Trevor, right?"

"No, Josh. He slipped on the soccer ball and landed on his arm. I think it's broken," she explained frantically.

"Oh my! Ok, yes, I'll be there right away. Can you put ice on his arm before I get there?" Somehow I managed to draw from my first aid training and spout the instructions without too much conscious thought.

I arrived in about half the time it should have taken to drive there. I jumped out of the car and ran up the hill to see my child clutching his right arm. I removed the ice pack and analyzed his little extremity. The pain seemed to be excruciating, but I didn't see any obvious signs of a break. Without having Superman's X-ray vision power, I decided taking him to the ER was the best decision. I sent the other children on a task to find an object to use for a splint. Soon we were on our way to the hospital. Josh sported a stiff wooden ruler and bag of ice wrapped around his forearm.

The children's hospital nursing staff believed his arm was probably broken, but after two sets of X-rays, no fracture was found. Nearly four hours later we left with anti-inflammatories and pain medication. Josh's tiny arm was encompassed by ice packs and elastic bandages. By the size of the wrapping, he looked like he was trying to smuggle a machine gun under his arm. At least his pain was under control.

Later that evening I called Theresa to offer an update on Josh's status. She was relieved his arm was not broken, but there was still a hint of worry in her voice. After a long pause and a verbal exhale, she informed me of her plans to no longer babysit my boys. *What?* I panicked as her words hit my ears with enough force to knock over an elephant. This can't be happening (again). "But it was just an accident, and Josh didn't break his arm after all," I said pleadingly, hopeful to sway her decision.

"I know accidents can happen. But I cannot handle the stress of having other people's children in my care with the possibility of something going wrong. I'm not even sure my homeowner's insurance would cover such an incident," Theresa explained. "I've decided not to babysit at all."

I assured her I would never sue for something my child induced, but it did not change her mind. It was final: we were left with no babysitter . . . again.

CHAPTER 17

Second Grade Introductions

Between the three of us parents and my recruited mother, we finagled our schedules to cover the summer babysitting needs. My mom was not excited about being tied up babysitting every Saturday, but she finally agreed when presented with enough monetary motivation. (It's amazing how receptive people become when money is involved.) It wasn't my ideal choice to work weekends, but the bills wouldn't pay themselves. Initially our hectic schedule increased Trevor's anxiety, but in time he accepted the unexpected and the constantly changing schedule. We made it through that summer. But little did we know life was about to change drastically.

A few days before school started, we were invited to tour the classroom and meet the second grade teacher. The visit benefited Trevor more than me since I had already met Mrs. Reno. I prepared him for this year and prayed he could break the silent cycle. But no amount of preparation can ensure one hundred percent success when it comes to selective mutism. The anxiety trumped normal life and played by its own rules. We determined the best approach for a positive outcome was to have a plan. If Trevor knew what to expect and what was expected of him, he handled the anxiety better. So, for weeks I reminded Trevor he would be in class with mostly different children than last year. Many were not aware of his verbal issues. I knew how badly Trevor wanted to communicate with his friends, and this helped with his determination.

"Now is the best time for a change," I told him. Then, I provided Trevor with a scenario of how an interaction might play out. "Sweetie, if you just start talking to someone in your class, they will have no idea you didn't talk before. So, they won't think anything of it. Even if it is someone who knows you, they probably won't remember how you struggled to find your voice before."

"What if they do make a big deal about it?" Trevor asked apprehensively.

"Then you can reply to them by saying, 'I just didn't have anything to say last year, but I've always been able to talk, just like you.' Or you can tell them you're older now and felt it was time."

Trevor nodded in acceptance, obviously pleased by my offered responses.

As we entered the classroom for our visit, Mrs. Reno spotted us nearly immediately. She smiled and waved from across the room. But she did not approach. Instead, she casually called out to Trevor, saying, "You can wander around the room and find your nametag on one of the desks. That will be your assigned seat when school starts."

Trevor smiled back, then proceeded to follow her instructions. Other children mingled with their parents. They pointed to the colorful posters hanging on the wall and plopped down into the bean bag chairs near the bookshelf in the corner of the room. I made my way over to Mrs. Reno. Trevor found an easel. He picked up the dry paintbrush, then proceeded to mime out a painting. I imagined the masterpiece he was creating in his mind when Mrs. Reno broke the silence. "He seems to be managing himself ok. I figured it was best to allow him to approach me rather than the other way around. It's less threatening that way."

"Great idea, that might help him feel more comfortable and not forced," I admitted, impressed already by Mrs. Reno's compassion and empathy.

As we chatted briefly, Trevor finished his mock painting, then moseyed over to a stack of games. He ran his finger down the edges of the boxes, pausing on one toward the bottom. When he glanced up in our direction, he caught my gaze. Mrs. Reno must have read his body language because she announced, "You'll find out in class how you can earn game time. So, if you see something you'd like to play, all you have to do is work for it." They exchanged smiles. Trevor abandoned the games and approached us. One of the other children overheard the teacher's statement and quizzed for more information.

"How do we earn game time?" The blonde-haired boy asked.

"Turn your homework in on time, help out in class, or doing something nice for someone else are a few ways to earn credits for free time, which includes playing games," the seasoned teacher replied.

"I love that idea," I said. "What a wonderful way to reinforce positive behavior."

"It has worked well in the past. And I feel it prepares them for the future, starts them off with a good work ethic," Mrs. Reno explained.

Then, the blonde boy turned to Trevor and asked, "Hey, where's your seat?"

Trevor shrugged his shoulders in reply and began to peruse the nametags on the desks. The blonde kid skipped happily around the desks and across the room to his assigned location. Then, he cheerfully announced for Trevor's benefit, "Here's my seat!"

Trevor spotted his name and tapped the desk in ownership with his hand. The blonde boy, apparently inquisitive by nature, questioned Trevor again. "What's your name? I'm Zach."

The boys stood about ten feet away from me, but I still heard the one-sided conversation without strain. I cringed inside and apparently outside, too, because Mrs. Reno responded, "Just give him time, Mom."

Then, I heard a faint "Trevor." I gulped down my surprise and turned quickly toward the boys. I searched for confirmation on whether I had heard my child talk or if it was Zach who read Trevor's nametag. But I missed the opportunity. They walked together to the other side of the room, out of earshot.

"Did you just hear Trevor say his name? Or did Zach read Trevor's nametag?" I asked the slender, warm-eyed woman.

"I didn't hear it, sorry," she answered honestly. "But I'm sure he'll be fine. He's already fitting in and interacting now, I am sure it will be no time before he is talking in class."

Hope and excitement arose. I may have heard Trevor talk for the first time in school. But then again, maybe my mind had played tricks on me. Did I dare ask my child? No, I knew that would be the wrong way to handle this situation. I didn't want to set him back in his progress with overcoming selective mutism. I learned that patience was always the best choice with this disorder.

On the ride home from the classroom tour, I quizzed Trevor on his new friend. "What did that boy say his name was?"

"Zach," he replied easily.

"He seems talkative and friendly."

"Yea," was the only response from my back seat.

"Does he know your name?" I asked sneakily.

"Yea."

Hmm, my beating-around-the-bush technique failed. I supposed that was what I got for asking yes-or-no questions. Now, how could I find out if Trevor spoke to the boy without bringing direct attention to his speaking? I resigned to the obvious answer: I don't. Anything I said at that point would be a blatant attempt, and Trevor would see right through it. Instead I focused on a discussion about the new school year and new possibilities. The moment we arrived home, Trevor jumped out of the car eagerly. He ran inside the house to tell his brother all about his new classroom and the friend he had met. My investigative opportunity jumped out the door with him. I was left wondering if he had used his voice or not.

PART 3

Winning The War On Selective Mutism

CHAPTER 18

Trevor Talks!

The few days leading up to the new school year were emotionally charged. Both boys were excited and eagerly anticipated this year of change. Josh was in another school, and Trevor had a new teacher. But they also were apprehensive about their impending first school day. This apprehension manifested itself as short tempers in each child. I attempted to be as understanding as possible with their bickering at one another. I empathized with their anxiousness toward all the changes, but secretly I had to admit it was times like these that made me jealous of parents with only one child. Not that I would trade either of my boys, but there was an allure in not having to deal with the sibling rivalry. The common occurrence of stomping feet and slammed doors was not my idea of quality time with either of my sons. And it got more frequent as they aged.

There was screaming from the boys' bedroom, which echoed down the hallway, followed by a loud thud. Praying one of my boys had not body-slammed the other into a concussion, I ran down the hall in fearful response. Throwing open their bedroom door, I quickly scanned the room to ensure both boys were coherent and still breathing. Wide, frightened eyes stared back at me as they each stood still, rooted to the floor. "What the hell is going on in here?" I yelled, anger swelling as I discovered they were fine.

Both boys argued their blame at the same time and sounded like a jumbled "he did it" in stereo.

Still confused and unable to comprehend either of their ramblings, I finally snapped again. "Stop it! Stop shouting! Now, tell me what that thud was!" In hindsight I realize screaming at my children to stop screaming was probably not the best parenting decision. But my emotions were calling the shots at that specific moment in time.

Josh was the first to answer. "The bed broke."

Well, sure enough, the end of Trevor's bed was off the rail and on the floor. How had I not noticed the slanting surface when I first entered the room? Trevor interjected, "Josh made me do it, he pushed me!"

"I did not, you kept jumping on my bed, I just made you move!" Josh countered in defense.

"You pushed me off your bed!" Trevor screamed, as if he had a right to be on Josh's bed in the first place.

"Ok, ok, guys, stop arguing," I managed to say with less volume or anger. "Let's see if we can fix it." I bent down and investigated the damage; it was an easy fix. After I put the boys to work on lifting the mattress together, we managed to slide the rail back into place and fix the broken bed. If only other life problems were as easy to repair.

I gave the boys the typical "don't jump on the furniture" lecture, and then we embraced in encouraging hugs. Watching TV seemed a better alternative than allowing them to pick up where they left off with their argument in their room. The three of us joined Nick (who, having just entered the house, missed all the commotion) in the family room for some togetherness time in front of the television.

The first school day arrived, and everyone arose easily in anticipation of the event. Josh already had his backpack ready and waiting, filled with pens, pencils, spiral notebooks, and folders. Trevor followed his brother's lead and also placed his backpack near the front door, but his contents were quite different as a second grader. Tissue boxes, glue sticks, scissors, crayons, and coloring pencils were among the items taking up residence in his bag. I always loved the first school day because the boys were happy. It reminded me of the beginning of a vacation with all the excitement, positive energy, and shared laughter over the simplest incidents. Times like these helped me appreciate having two children. Suddenly I felt sorry for those parents with only one child. They never experienced the loving sibling interactions.

After I dropped Josh off at the middle school, Trevor and I drove to the elementary building. "Do you want me to drop you off in the drop-off zone, or do you want to walk in with me today?"

"I'll go with you," Trevor answered, the apprehension obvious in his voice as he scanned the school grounds and took in all the people.

The drop-off zone was filled to the street, so I was relieved Trevor chose to go with me. An office worker stood in the road, patrolling the cars to control the chaos. As I drove around her, she shouted and pointed toward the back of the long line in the drop-off zone. Through my open window I shouted, "I'm a worker, going inside." She nodded, then motioned me to the front staff parking lot. Volunteering has its benefits.

Soon I discovered Trevor no longer wanted to hold my hand while walking into the building. Was this a positive reflection of his issue? I determined he was either more mature or too embarrassed to be witnessed with a parental chaperone. Then I realized both reasons were probably true. Josh went through something similar with being embarrassed by public affection. But Trevor always appreciated the handholding and seemed to have gained courage by it. So, maybe today was a good sign. A smile crept onto my face after I came to this conclusion. This was going to be a good school year!

After I signed in at the front office and received my volunteer badge, we headed for the second grade classroom. Children congested the hallway. They ogled at the walls as if touring a museum and admiring artistic masterpieces. There were posters hung outside the classrooms. Some were inspirational, and some were humorous. Several children pointed and laughed at one poster. It displayed a cat hanging from a tree limb with bold letters that read, HANG IN

THERE! The teacher across the hall began motioning for her kids to come inside, which reduced the crowd substantially. Then, Mrs. Reno stepped into her doorway and announced, "You will have all school year to read the posters. Please come inside before the bell rings. You don't want to be tardy on your first day." With that instruction the entire group of giggling second graders quickly changed their focus and made their way inside the room, Trevor following behind the pack.

After a quick command from Mrs. Reno to find their seats, she turned her attention to me. "Thank you for coming in today to help. I appreciate the chance to get a head start. The copy machine should be available since most of the volunteers for other teachers won't be starting until next week."

"It's my pleasure," I said. "It gives me peace of mind that Trevor's first day will be a little less stressful, knowing I'm in the building."

"Yes, great idea. But I have a feeling everything's going to go just fine. He seems to be fitting in well already," she stated, jutting her chin in Trevor's direction.

As I glanced toward that side of the room, I spotted Trevor engaged with another child. From my vantage point I could not tell if he was talking or just listening. But with his history of not speaking, I figured it was the latter. Either way, I couldn't hover over him all day. It was time for this momma bird to push her fledgling out of the nest.

Toward the end of the school day, Mrs. Reno caught me before I entered her classroom. "I wanted to talk to you without Trevor hearing," she whispered. "You will be surprised, but Trevor talked in class."

"What!" I exclaimed, louder than I intended. I lowered my voice and head and attempted to control my surprised excitement. "He talked? Really? To you?"

"He talked to another boy in class, but he also responded to me when I called on him once. See, Mom? No need for worry, he's just fine," Mrs. Reno declared with shining eyes and a warm smile.

Relief flooded through me, and my heart pounded in response to the shocking news. I disbelieved he would talk so soon. I assumed he would need another school year and feared he may never find his voice. But to start talking on day one of second grade? I never expected such a reaction. After a brief exchange of bewilderment, we both entered the room together. Soon, the bell rang, and day one was complete—a day that would go down in history. A day that changed our lives forever. I couldn't wait to talk to Trevor about this amazing accomplishment. Logically I knew it might embarrass him, so I drew in a deep breath and resolved to wait until he brought it up.

In the car Trevor excitedly announced, "I met a couple of new friends, and I talked to one of them."

I swallowed down my instinct to sing aloud with excitement about his verbal accomplishment and decided to respond calmly. "That's wonderful, honey. I knew you could make friends quickly. And who wouldn't like you? You're awesome!"

His return smile confirmed he was proud of his accomplishment. While the dialogue was open, I probed further. "Was it hard to talk to new friends?"

"Yea, it was hard at first," Trevor admitted. "Especially when Brady heard me. He remembered last year I didn't talk, so he was kinda surprised. But I told him I've always talked, just like him. I just didn't have anything to say last year. He laughed at that."

Fear struck when I heard the words "he laughed." I was worried my child might be embarrassed by the other boy's response. But his smile did not waver. Today, he was strong and handled the pressure. I prayed tomorrow would be the same.

CHAPTER 19

Overcoming Selective Mutism

Over the next week Trevor's voice continued to be heard in class only by a select few. But this was such a huge improvement over his previous years of barely saying hi to his teacher. My prayers had been answered. My child was finally talking! There were many days when he still came home stressed, but not as severely stressed as in the past. The daily beatings to the back of my seat were no longer Trevor's primary emotional outlet the moment he entered the car. Instead he bottled his anger up over a few days, then released it all at once. I'm not sure it was a healthier solution, but that was how Trevor had learned to cope with his anxiety in his less than eight years of existence.

Volunteer day arrived again, and I couldn't wait to hear all about Trevor using his voice from his teacher. Upon entering the classroom, I spotted Mrs. Reno busy with a student, so I patiently waited by her desk.

A light brown-haired boy approached me. "You're Trevor's mom, aren't you?"

"Yes, I am," I replied to the slightly oversized child and watched as he pushed his glasses back up his nose.

"I didn't think Trevor knew how to talk. He didn't do it last year. When did he learn?" asked the inquisitive boy.

"He's always known how to talk, he just was a little . . . shy last year, that's all. But I think he's feeling more comfortable now," I explained in words that would make sense to this second grader, who was confused by Trevor's change in demeanor.

"Brady, please take your seat," Mrs. Reno said to the boy with all the questions.

Ah, that was Brady. He did look a little familiar, but Trevor didn't talk about him much last year. I supposed Brady took more of an interest in Trevor this year because of his verbal change. Trevor seemed to enjoy Brady's attention, for which I was truly thankful. My fears about him being embarrassed by Brady's constant bombardment of questions subsided.

I watched the two boys exchange big smiles and pleasantries. Then, Brady took his seat three desks away from my son. The interaction warmed my heart, and for a brief moment I felt like my son was normal and was finally fitting in. But his stressful outbursts continued at home, especially toward his brother. This quickly reminded me he was not fully normal. Our focus changed from encouraging Trevor's comfort of using his voice to anger management. All along he had struggled to cope with stress, but his selective mutism trumped the anger issues. Or maybe we could only tackle one issue at a time and had overlooked his misbehavior? I researched child anger management online and found several sources for oppositional defiant disorder. While Trevor did not fit the symptoms entirely, the information helped. The last thing we wanted to do was take Trevor to another psychologist. At least not so soon after his recent accomplishment. He deserved time to adjust to this new behavior and adapt to his new life. I hoped in time his anger would also diminish as he learned to be social in school.

A few months into the school year proved Trevor's achievement of speaking in class was more than a fluke. It was as if he no longer had selective mutism, and I pondered the possibility. Can SM go away? Can it be cured? It seemed Trevor had done that as he no longer suffered from the crippling anxiety over using his voice in public. Life was . . . normal. Or so it appeared.

November of that year, Nick and I married. Trevor and Josh were a big part of the ceremony. I'll never forget when Nick proposed the summer prior. He assembled a family meeting after I said yes to his big question. He proceeded to propose to the boys, too. Nick felt they should have a voice in our union. Fortunately they accepted, and we officially became a family.

One evening not long after our wedding, my brother-in-law called from his deployment in Iraq. Josh and Trevor were his biggest fans; they were proud of their Army uncle. He received the care package we mailed, including Trevor's cute drawing of him in a jeep, and wanted to thank the boys personally. I thrust the phone into Trevor's direction, then instructed him to tell his Uncle Mike hi. The color instantly drained from his complexion, and his face froze in horror. His reaction confused me, and I stood there dumbfounded. Time seemed to switch into slow motion before my eyes. My husband grabbed the phone and handed it off to Josh as the scene unfolded, and I struggled to make sense of it. Nick then announced, "Uncle Mike can't talk long, he's calling from far away." Josh proceeded to chat affectionately with his uncle while I continued in my disbelief. What had happened? I thought Trevor was normal now. But that drastic, panicked reaction was far from normal.

After the phone call ended, I quizzed Trevor. "Sweetie, what happened? Why didn't you talk to Uncle Mike?"

Trevor's tiny shoulders raised and dropped in a shrug of uncertainty, and he shook his head. "I don't know," he admitted, then ran off to his bedroom to return to the computer game he had paused for the phone call.

With a bewildered look still plastered on my face, I turned to my husband for answers. "Do you have any idea what just happened?"

"I'm surprised you are surprised," he responded. "You know Trevor has selective mutism. Why did you push him to talk to Mike?"

"But he has been talking in school since the first day this year. I thought he was cured." As the words tumbled out of my mouth, the realization of my naiveté surfaced. There is no cure for selective mutism. Deep down I knew this to be true. We discussed the situation at length and agreed Trevor would always have this issue. Anxiety doesn't magically disappear.

The holidays approached, which meant less time for us and more time with the extended family. We joked that if it weren't for having to spend time with family, the holidays would be perfect. The actual time spent with our extended family wasn't really dreaded; it was the stress evoked by having to drive everywhere when we preferred being lazy at home. But traditions are important, and we felt we needed to teach those behaviors to our children. Plus, deep down there was this little nagging voice which said, *If I had to do it, then you have to do it.*

Visiting my mom was always a challenge, especially since my father had passed. Her home was not child-friendly. And the other grandchildren were older, so the boys had to entertain themselves. Josh and Trevor had a ton of toys and handheld electronic games they could play, but their endurance for visits was short. Within half an hour of arrival, they began whispering their pleadings.

"When are we leaving?"

After a dozen variations of this same question, I would finally surrender and graciously prepare for our departure. This visit was no different. Trevor kept pulling on my sweater to grab my attention. His face pleaded for us to leave. My mother picked up on the boys' restlessness and attempted to redirect their attention by engaging them in conversation.

"Josh, how's school going this year?" Josh was surprised to hear his grandmother say his name. He immediately froze with his body pushed against Trevor as he held him back from reaching the game clutched in his hand.

Josh answered, "Great."

Trevor stopped reaching for the game in Josh's possession, worried he may become the subject of Grandma's next question.

After a brief discussion about Josh's teacher and class, my mother moved on to her youngest grandson. "I've heard this year is special for you, Trevor. Have you made lots of new friends?"

The all-too-common paralyzed reaction appeared on Trevor's face when he realized he was now the focus of attention. With widened eyes he forced a quick nod, then diverted his gaze to the floor. My heart sank with disappointment. But my mother didn't miss a beat. She was used to this reaction from him and continued with the yes/no, closed-ended questions. Trevor slinked away behind his brother to escape the scrutiny, and my mom stopped the questions. The boys went to the other room and fetched their coats as I expressed my discouragement in Trevor's lack of speaking with my mother.

"I don't get it, Mom. He talks in school. Why can't he talk to you, his own grandmother, or his uncle or anyone else in our family?"

"Maybe he needs more time to get used to talking," my mom replied as she grasped at any answer that might console her own baby girl.

"I'm sorry. I know he loves you, Mom, but he has such a hard time breaking these secret rules he has set for himself. Since he's never talked to you, he's uncomfortable starting. In class, most of the kids are different than last year and don't know he didn't talk." As I spoke, the words began to make sense. Trevor always had invisible rules he followed. Not talking to my mother was one of those rules.

My mom switched the subject to something less intrusive. She was good at deflecting. When uncomfortable, she made a joke or changed the subject. This defensive reaction pained me more, and I realized how disappointed my mother was that Trevor didn't talk to her. Especially when made aware he spoke to strangers. I felt powerless to change the situation, so I offered a warm hug and a verbal "I love you" to my mom as we all crowded into the car and prepared to leave. Trevor waved his silent goodbye as we pulled out of the driveway, away from another failed communication attempt.

CHAPTER 20

School Presentations Read Aloud

After the winter break an announcement came home in Trevor's school packet about a big project the kids had been working on. Each child had chosen a country to study and was expected to read their report in front of the class. Parents were invited to attend the middle-of-the-day classroom event. Trevor told me about his chosen country of Denmark and described some of the details of the report he had been working on in class, but he had failed to mention anything about inviting parents to the classroom presentation.

I didn't want to miss a single moment in Trevor's life, so I was surprised he hadn't shared the event information. He should have known I would be more than eager to attend. As soon as this thought filtered to the forefront of my mind, I chuckled aloud. Obviously my child *did* know me well, which was exactly why he didn't tell me about the event. He hoped I wouldn't hear about it and therefore not attend. Ha! That was not going to happen.

Discussing the invitation with Trevor seemed the best approach for preparing him to expect me in the room while he read aloud to the other kids. An idea popped into my head. The teacher had mentioned that parents and grandparents were invited to hear the reports, so maybe my mother would attend also. Running this idea by Trevor first seemed like a responsible choice, but I was fearful he would say he didn't want her present. For a fleeting moment I considered sneaking her into the back of the room without Trevor knowing at all. But logically I decided to do what was best for my son, and I discussed it with him.

"Hey sweetie, I got an invitation from your teacher to attend the country class reports next week and was thinking about coming. Would you be ok with that?" I asked my child, easing into the next question resting on the tip of my tongue.

"Yea, I guess, but it'll be boring," he replied pretentiously.

"It might be interesting too," I countered.

"Yea, maybe." His hesitant response caused red flags to fling up in my mind. My child loved geography, so this event would be far from boring for him. Trevor and his brother played a game at home my husband created, which sparked their love for geography. They would spot a location on our globe, spin it around a few times, and then ask the other person to find said location in a certain time frame. I was always amazed at how quickly they pinpointed the exact area. So, Trevor's indifference struck me as odd, and my skin tingled at his apprehension. A new approach was necessary to ease into the big question of inviting my mother to his event.

I quickly came up with a strategy to redirect the focus away from his speaking aloud and suggested, "Hearing about all those other countries might be fun since each person will be reading about a different place. I bet the other kids will appreciate having someone to listen to all their hard work."

Trevor considered this proposal for a couple of minutes, then replied, "Yea, that might be cool. If you want to come, I'm ok with that."

Was now the time for my next question, or would it cause my child a setback? While I internally debated this dilemma, Trevor moved past the idea of my presence at his event and began brainstorming ideas for his presentation. His excitement grew in his voice as he suggested, "Maybe we could get cookies to share for my display? The kind of cookies they eat in Denmark. One of the kids is planning on bringing pizza, he's doing Italy."

"Oh yes, we could get cookies or maybe Danish pastries. That's a great idea, Trevor," I proudly admitted. "But how is your classmate planning to keep the pizza warm?"

He shrugged his little shoulders and wore a blank expression, which gave me the impression he had no idea. Possibly his classmate hadn't thought that far in advance either. It was then I decided to dive right into the dreaded question. "I'm sure your grandma would love to taste foods from different countries, maybe I can invite her to come too?"

"Sure," he hastily agreed while his mind was still preoccupied with the pizza issue. I avoided discussing the implications of having his grandmother present during his speech-reading moment. It was better to redirect his focus on the fun with the food and the other kids' speeches rather than on him.

We chatted about other ideas for his country display. We both enjoyed the anticipation of his potential project, and he decided Danish pastries would be best to share with his classmates. As we worked out a time frame on when and how I would bring his food on the day of the event, I avoided mentioning my mother again. With any luck he wouldn't even notice she was present.

Over the next week Trevor worked diligently on his project. I watched as he colored large squares on a piece of white typing paper. Between the red colored squares a white T began to form. I jokingly asked, "Why are you making the Switzerland flag?"

A slightly panicked expression crossed his face, but then he realized my playfulness and giggled out his response. "The Denmark flag does look a little like Switzerland, doesn't it? But the Switzerland flag is just a plus sign, not a letter T," he explained confidently.

Yes, I knew better than to challenge my second grader to a geography question. He would win against me every time, hands down. I liked to think he excelled in the subject rather than admit to my lack of knowledge. But honestly, geography was never my strong suit. And I was thankful my husband influenced the boys and encouraged their love for the subject. Trevor finished coloring his Denmark flag, then he worked on his table sign. I loved watching him color, especially when he created a masterpiece. Trevor had such a creative flare, even at his young age. After he folded the paper in fourths, he then opened it up and smoothed out the creases. He followed up with writing "Denmark" in a middle section of the paper. After he colored in the letters and made them bold, he refolded the paper into a freestanding triangular shape reminding me of a Toblerone candy bar, which created his table sign. I was impressed by his design.

"Wow, that's a neat trick. How did you know to do that?" I asked.

"Mrs. Reno showed us in class. Everybody has to make one," he replied, unaware that I gave him credit for the creative construction before I knew his source. "Now, I gotta write out my paper that I have to read. But I'm worried I won't be able to write it clear enough," he admitted nervously.

"How about a typed paper?" I proposed. Judging by the gleam in his eyes and the huge smile he gave at my suggestion, I realized he heard more words than I had said. Instead, my child heard, "Why don't I type your paper for you?" I had not intended to offer to do it for him, so I added quickly, "You can type it. The practice would be good for you."

His smile wavered, and he replied, "But you type so much faster. And I like to watch how fast your fingers move on the keyboard." I was aware he was buttering me up to do his work for him, but his little boy's charms still affected me. Darn it, how did he have so much power over me? His happiness meant everything to me.

After I typed his single-page paper, we finished getting everything ready for the big day. We shopped for the Danish pastries, which was quite enjoyable mostly because we did it together. I always appreciated it when he was in a cheerful mood. After we discussed my arrival time (which would be a few minutes before the event), with his bag of goodies, his plans were in place. I hoped being prepared would help suppress his anxieties. He handled stressful situations like this presentation best when he knew what to expect and what was expected of him. The one thing I purposefully failed to remind him of was his grandmother's planned attendance. I didn't hide it from him, but I didn't bring it to his attention either. With any luck maybe he wouldn't notice her there.

The morning came quickly, as most mornings do for a non-morning person. Trevor and Josh were arguing already, and we hadn't even had breakfast—not a good start. But Trevor's emotions were high with the stress of the big day, so after taking a large drink of my coffee, I ventured down the hallway to their room to play mediator.

"Morning, boys!" I announced as cheerfully as I could muster on only one swig of coffee. "Josh, Trevor has a big day today with his presentation, so maybe we could be a little more understanding?" I suggested to my eldest, hopeful he was in an obliging mood.

"Oh yea, you got your speech today," he said, glancing in Trevor's direction.

"It's not a speech, it's a presentation," Trevor corrected, as if there was much difference.

"Whatever, you still have to get up in front of the class and talk, so it's like a speech," Josh explained.

I clenched my teeth tightly together and cringed at Josh's analogy. If Trevor considered it a speech, he could lose his nerve with reading his report aloud.

But luckily Trevor responded in agreement with his brother. "Oh, that makes sense. Yea, I got a speech today," he said.

"How about I heat up some Toaster Strudels for breakfast?" I quickly interjected, hopeful to redirect their attention as we prepared for the school day. "Eggs and strudels, is there anything better?"

"I don't want any eggs," Trevor replied. "Just the Toaster Strudel."

"But sweetie, you need something a little more substantial than just a Toaster Strudel."

"Ok, then I'll eat two Toaster Strudels."

"Um, it doesn't work like that. You need some protein," I said. "Especially for your big day."

"Ok, I'll eat a little bit of scrambled eggs," he said, finally settling. "But I don't want any yellows."

"I'll take scrambled eggs too," Josh eagerly added.

109

Off to the kitchen I headed, pleased as the boys chatted happily behind me in their room.

After breakfast was consumed and the dishes were stacked in the sink, we headed out the door. Since Josh's school started earlier than Trevor's, we dropped him off first. Trevor didn't want to ride the bus today since he had so many items to carry for his presentation. So, we took a little detour through the local park and killed time before his school started. The winding road through the wooded park was relaxing even though the trees stared back at us with their bare branches. I pulled up next to the pond, and Trevor prepared to get out. "Oh sweetie, it's too chilly today to walk around outside. We'll just enjoy the view from the warmth of the car, ok?" I glanced around for any signs of wildlife, but winter was not the best season to catch a glimpse of them wandering around. The trees rustled their branches in response to the cold wind blowing through the area, and I noticed an object on the other side of the pond. "Look over there. Is that a turtle?" I asked, unable to make out the dark object next to the water's edge.

"What are you talking about? I don't see a turtle," Trevor responded, confused as to where I was referring.

"Over there, that dark thing next to the water. It's not moving, but it looks like a turtle."

"Um, are you talking about that big rock?" he asked, baffled by how I could confuse a rock for a turtle.

"Oh, is that a rock? Well, it's in a turtle shape," I said, defending my initial guess.

"I've never seen a turtle the size of a car before," Trevor said with a chuckle.

"It's not that big. Here, let's drive over there and take a closer look."

After I drove the car around the pond to the other side, the size of the rock grew. "Hmm, it didn't look as big from over there," I said while pointing behind us.

After our giggling fest it was time for school. So, off we headed toward Trevor's big day.

I parked in the main lot, then helped Trevor carry in all his items for his project. He didn't act nervous yet, but I felt it was best to not mention his impending speech. Instead, I gave him a sign wave of "I love you" and told him I'd be back soon. He smiled sweetly as he returned the ASL sign. My heart sang. Shared moments like these would stay with me all my days.

Later that day I picked up my mother, and we drove together to see the children's country presentations at the elementary school. My stomach began doing acrobatic moves in anticipation of Trevor's big moment, so I shared this concern with my mom. She, too, was nervous, but it was more of a nervous excitement about hearing her grandson talk in person for the first time. My fear was he would freeze and be unable to read his report. But I had to remain positive. He could do it; he was brave.

After we signed in at the office, my mother and I made our way down the hall to the second grade classroom. We sported our official visitor nametags proudly. The music bellowed as it drifted through the hallway and guided us to the correct room. Without the need to read the numbers on the door, we found the room easily as the commotion screamed, *The party is here!* We entered the classroom, and I spotted the spectator area to the right. There were a dozen chairs positioned into two rows. I glanced to the left and saw the children's desks were separated, which allowed a path for walking around each of their country displays. I spotted Trevor toward the back. He milled around his desk and ensured everything was set up exactly right. I directed my mother to a chair in the front row while Mrs. Reno guided the children into their positions and made final preparations for the festivities. Several other parental figures filtered into the room and joined my mother and me in the seating area. The air vibrated with contagious excitement, and I couldn't stop smiling in response. Soon the music ended, and we were left with a brief silence, which settled the classroom full of children immediately. There were a couple of hushed sounds in the back from one child to another, and then Mrs. Reno broke the silence.

"Thank you all for coming to our country presentation today. I realize you have busy lives, so we feel honored to have you here. The children have all worked so hard on their reports, and I am proud of each and every one of them. I'm sure you will enjoy hearing about their countries as we travel around the world together." After Mrs. Reno's introduction there was a brief round of applause. Then, she continued, "We have a lot of reports to hear, so please refrain from clapping until after every speech is read. Now, let us start from the other side of the world as we visit China." A small girl stood up behind her desk at the mention of her chosen country and began reading from her paper. This continued for several more country reports until finally we arrived at Europe. For a moment I worried my beating heart would drown out the children's voices but soon realized only I could hear the pounding. My mom seemed to be thoroughly enjoying hearing all the young speakers and listened intently with a gleam of excitement in her eye.

Finally, the main reason for our attendance arrived: it was my child's turn. As soon as the student next to him sat down, Trevor stood on cue. He held his paper up in front of his face and began reading his report. The sound of his little voice trickled through the room and immediately pulled on my heartstrings. The tears that had gathered at my lower eyelids in anticipation of this moment now flowed freely down my cheeks. My sniffles caught the attention of the parent next to me. She smiled and whispered, oblivious to his struggles, "They're so cute at this age, aren't they?" I nodded with a feeble smile, then continued to fight off my emotions. I didn't comprehend a single word my child spoke, but I heard every syllable and sound emitted from his lips. He was doing it—he was speaking in public and most importantly in front of his grandmother. I glanced to my left and watched my mother's eyes as they lit up in approval of hearing her grandson speak aloud. I wasn't sure how she held it together so well because no tears stained her cheeks. Maybe that was best for Trevor. She was managing to reduce the enormity of this moment into a smile. Why hadn't I inherited her self-control?

After his speech Trevor sat quickly. He analyzed an invisible object in his hands and avoided eye contact with the audience. It was a blessing he didn't look up immediately, which gave me time to recover. As the speeches neared North America, Trevor chanced a glance in our direction. I smiled proudly, motioning a small "I love you" sign. His sweet grin warmed my heart. The moment he noticed his grandmother next to me, he quickly looked away toward the boy speaking about Canada.

After the presentations were read, everyone toured the individual country displays at their leisure. My mother and I made a beeline for Denmark, hopeful to catch Trevor before he made his way around the world. He stood discreetly next to his desk, and we greeted him with hugs. As I overheard my mother telling Trevor how proud she was of him, more tears tugged at my eyelids. I took a deep breath and sucked them back in, then managed to face my child again. The smile came easily—I was proud of his accomplishment. This was a triumphant day, one I had been unsure would ever materialize.

As my mother and I left the school building, emotions overcame me once again. Tears of joy gushed down my cheeks. There was no closing the floodgates this time. Mom consoled me with a light pat on my back. I was thankful she understood but confused as to why she wasn't bawling along with me. Then, as I glanced into her eyes, I saw her tears threatening to break free and shatter her stalwart image. Somehow that helped me pull it together. I couldn't cause my mother to look weak when she had tried desperately to be strong. I took a deep breath, then recovered enough that my crying stopped. I drove her home, and after our goodbyes I pulled out of her driveway with tear-stained cheeks once again.

CHAPTER 21

Leo the Lion Finds His Voice

The rest of the second grade passed by without any further hurdles. Disappointingly, though, Trevor didn't come out of his shell with my mother. It was as if this invisible wall of rules still blocked him from talking to close family members. But the end of the school year brought promise. Trevor spoke in class to a few friends, and it appeared as if he no longer suffered from selective mutism. Granted, he wasn't overly chatty by any means, but he spoke enough to fit in and appeared "normal."

Toward the end of the school year, the director of the gifted program approached me during one of my volunteer days. Every second grade student was tested for their IQ score, which determined qualification into the gifted program for third through fifth grades. Trevor's score was slightly below their requirements but close enough to be considered. Since he had an older brother who was in the gifted program prior, Trevor had a little leverage. So, the director asked me if I wanted Trevor retested for the program. Initially, I was ecstatic and wanted my child recognized for his intellect. I believed most parents would be proud to have their child in an excellerated program for only a select few. But Trevor wasn't just any child. He struggled with anxieties and had only recently begun to overcome his selective mutism. No, this was something I could not take lightly and needed to contemplate further.

After I talked with my husband and Trevor's father, we decided it was in Trevor's best interest not to pursue another change in his life at this time. Third grade would be enough stress for him, and we feared one more added anxiety on top of it could hinder his progression with his disorder. I wanted to talk to Trevor about it and ask his opinion, but the other two adults advised me against this idea. That would put more stress on Trevor. So, we embraced the idiom: what he doesn't know won't hurt him.

I couldn't let Trevor go without him being informed of the situation. I avoided the details to prevent his stress from being triggered, choosing my words carefully while we briefly chatted.

"Hey, sweetie, I wanted you to know you scored amazingly well on the IQ portion they gave everyone during the schoolwide testing a few weeks back."

"I didn't know I was tested for that," he replied honestly.

"Yes, it was part of another test you were given. Anyway, you are one smart cookie."

A smile crept across his face in response to the information and extended all the way to mine.

"Do you remember the gifted program Josh was in? The one where he had to leave his regular class one day every week and go to another school with a group of students to do extra work?" I asked.

"Yea, kinda," Trevor said.

"Well, you were borderline for being accepted into that program—that's how smart you are, kiddo. But luckily, you won't have to do it. So, you won't have to leave your classroom and miss a day of school or do extra work. It was always a hassle for Josh to try to make up the homework he missed."

"Oh yea, that's good. I don't think I'd like to have to go to another school every week," he said in agreement. At that admission the conversation was over. Neither of us spoke of it again, and my guilt lifted.

During spring cleaning one day, I reached under Trevor's bed, and my hand touched something fuzzy and soft. As I grasped the object, I pulled out Leo the Lion, the stuffed animal hand puppet. Memories of Trevor's struggles from preschool resurfaced, and I couldn't help but smile at his progress since then. Leo had finally found his voice this year. Suddenly, an idea popped into my head. While Trevor played contently with his playdough, I approached and mentioned about finding the hand puppet. We both reminisced about his younger years as if he had grown wise and old in that short period of time. After the shared moment I presented my idea.

"Maybe I could sign you out of school early one day, and we could go to the preschool to give Leo back to Mrs. Richmond. Since he's found his voice," I added.

"Yea, that would be cool," Trevor replied with slight enthusiasm in his head nod.

"You could write her a letter about how Leo found his voice this year and thank her for lending him to you," I suggested.

The gleam in his eye told me he loved my idea and was ready to face his fears head-on. An overwhelming rush of pride swept through me. My baby was growing up.

Surprisingly, Trevor put down his playdough and began working on Mrs. Richmond's letter right away. He found a blank piece of notebook paper and a pencil and brought them into the kitchen. I had moved to my next cleaning project of loading the dishwasher. He sat at the table near me, then stared at the blank paper for a few moments. After he wrote "Mrs. Richmond" at the top of the page, he stared again.

"How should I start it? I don't know what to say," he said.

"Maybe that's how you should start, by telling Mrs. Richmond you're not sure where to begin, that so much has happened since she gave you Leo," I offered.

"Yea, that sounds good." He nodded as he wrote those exact words.

After we probed his memory and he decided what he wanted to convey, we wrote the letter together. He read it back to me, and I couldn't fight off the tears that collected in my eyes while I heard his sweet, innocent voice. Trevor glanced up and witnessed my emotion. Thankfully, he smiled. He understood these were tears of joy.

"Maybe you can *read* your letter to Mrs. Richmond instead of just handing it to her. It might mean more to her to hear the words," I suggested, hopeful I hadn't pushed him too hard.

As he contemplated this idea, a smile crept across his face. "Yea, I'm sure she would love that," he said.

Relief soared through me, and I was so pleased my suggestion didn't shut him down. He had evolved and learned to handle the anxiety. I could not have been prouder.

I arranged to pick him up early from school two days later. When the day came, we rode on our journey to the preschool. My sweaty hands made it difficult to hold the steering wheel, which reminded me of my nervousness building inside. "How are you doing, babe?" I asked my brave boy sitting in the passenger seat.

"Ok" was the only word he managed to utter. Butterflies fluttered in my stomach at his response, or lack of. If I felt this nervous, how did Trevor feel? As I thought about his anxiousness, I realized now was not the best time for his feelings to be discussed. He was facing the biggest feat of his life since the time he read his speech in front of the classroom of people.

"You'll do fine, sweetie. Mrs. Richmond will be so happy to get Leo back and to know how important she was in your life. She might even cry tears of joy like I did." I prepared him for her possible emotional reaction, hoping it helped him to be prepared for what to anticipate. He handled tasks better when he knew exactly what to expect.

"Yea, she might cry," he agreed, "since you did."

Whew, he was prepared. A smile spread across my face, and my eyes lit up as I thought about the moment at hand. Excitement won out as the strongest emotion.

After we pulled into the parking lot of the preschool, I found a space close to the connecting sidewalk and parked the car. I wiped my sweaty palms onto my pant legs, and then we both took a deep breath and exited the vehicle. Trevor stood tall, confident, and strong as he entered the building. His body language helped me feel confident and strong too—amazing how much a child's emotional state can impact an adult's.

We stopped at the office front desk, and I asked where we could find Mrs. Richmond. After I briefly explained the reason for our visit was to return her hand puppet, the receptionist offered to give it to Mrs. Richmond. I then explained that Trevor wanted to read a letter to her personally.

"She's in the playroom right now with her class. You can go on back," the office lady said pleasantly.

As we passed through the first two rooms, memories flooded my thoughts. I had helped teach in these classrooms more than once and served as a substitute when the lead teacher was off. I glanced down at my son and saw only determination on his face. He ignored any reminiscing and focused on the task at hand. This was going to happen.

We found Mrs. Richmond watching as the children played on the tree slide. I finally managed to get her attention with the sound of the door closing. I motioned for her to come over, and she immediately approached us. But as soon as Trevor began to hand her Leo, she realized the importance of today's visit. She held up one finger and motioned for us to wait a moment. After she indicated to the other teacher in the room that she was stepping out, she guided us into the small hallway right outside of the noisy playroom.

The moment the glass doors closed, the sound reduced to a low background noise that filtered away from our forethoughts. Trevor once again held out Leo toward Mrs. Richmond. This time she accepted the lion hand puppet with slight confusion.

I tried desperately to keep my mouth shut and allow my child to guide this meeting. But the quiet moment was nearly more than I could handle. Finally, Mrs. Richmond broke the silence.

"You're giving me a hand puppet?" she asked, still puzzled.

Trevor unfolded his letter, then began to read:

"Mrs. Richmond,
I'm not sure where to begin, so I'll start with, thank you. Thank you for my good memories of preschool in 2001 to 2002. Thank you for sharing your Teddy Grahams with me back then. I still remember your kindness. Thank you for trying to help me find the

courage to speak. And most of all, thank you for lending me your good friend Leo. You told me Leo couldn't find his voice and that I should keep him until he learned to talk. Well, here we are today. Leo has found his voice! I appreciated having him these past three years, but now I think he belongs with you. Maybe he can help another child or just make your class smile.

You were a special person in my life and helped me more than you know. Thank you."

Amazingly, Mrs. Richmond didn't cry. But her huge smile and warm embrace spoke volumes of her emotion. This was a moment we would remember for a lifetime.

We chatted briefly for a few more minutes, but Mrs. Richmond's time was needed elsewhere, so we excused ourselves. The excitement of the experience was coursing through our veins, and both Trevor and I needed an outlet for our high. We exited the building with big smiles on our faces and babbled nearly incoherently about the event.

"Let's go to the park and walk around a bit," I suggested, hopeful the exercise would help us burn off the extra adrenaline. As we pulled into the park, I spotted the ducks and geese near the water's edge of the pond. "Hey, my lunch box from earlier is still in the back seat. I think I have some bread left from my sandwich. Do you want to feed the ducks?" I asked.

"Yea, that would be cool," Trevor said.

I dug around on the floorboard behind the driver's seat until my hand grasped the container holding the remains of my lunch. Sure enough, there was plenty of wheat bread left on my half-eaten peanut butter sandwich. I handed Trevor some of the crust of the wheat bread, and we headed toward the birds.

The bread caused quite a ruckus with the animals. It was as if a power switch had been turned on and they all came to life. They flew in from the other side of the pond toward the food source. Trevor took a couple of steps backward to clear himself from the feasting frenzy, then tossed a few more pieces of the wheat crust away from the big flock. The birds responded immediately and gathered in the new area to fight for their share of crumbs.

"Wow, they're crazy," Trevor remarked as he watched the abundance of ruffled feathers in awe. Their squawking reminded me of the middle school band as they warmed up before a concert (or maybe even the actual concert of the young musicians as they played notes in the wrong key).

Trevor looked like a momma bird for a moment as several ducks waddled closely behind him and begged for more food. After the birds were fed the remaining wheat bread, we relocated quickly to avoid the vultures we had created.

I passed by a sign near the front of the pond and froze in place. The words read: DO NOT FEED THE WILDLIFE. Oh no, we just broke the law. My stomach plunged, and I nearly buckled over in fear. Trevor spotted the sign soon after, and he began laughing.

"Oops," he said between giggles. Then, he noticed my panicked expression and immediately attempted to console me. "It's ok, we didn't know. And the birds seemed to like it. Plus, we didn't really feed them very much bread."

He was right. We barely had enough crumbs to feed a tenth of the birds. And wheat is good for birds, right? Yes, I needed to pull myself together and stop stressing. These thoughts tumbled around in my brain for a moment, and then the emotions of the whole afternoon bubbled up to the surface and spilled out in the form of laughter with my child.

I added to the silliness of the situation and said, "Technically, are the ducks really that wild? I mean, they came right up to you, so they're kind of tame. The sign said, 'Don't feed the wildlife.' Did you see any *wild* animals?"

"Nope, they seemed pretty tame to me. And I didn't see any sign that said, 'Don't feed the tame life.'"

We both chuckled about our mistake the whole walk back to the car. It was a perfect release of emotion, the best way to burn off all the excess tension. We couldn't have planned a better outlet.

CHAPTER 22

Quiet Gestures Make Loud Impressions

The end of the school year came and went, which brought summer break into full swing. This was the first year we didn't have a babysitter lined up, so we struggled to finagle our schedules. The boys' dad and my husband agreed to cover a few days during the week. I bribed my mother into babysitting on Saturdays. The idea of extra cash for bingo easily persuaded her. With all the crazy, changed schedules, I managed to earn enough money to pay my bills that summer. Life was overwhelming, but at least Trevor began using his voice around others. Not yet to his grandmother, even though he spent nearly every Saturday at her home, but he wasn't hiding from her either as he did when he was smaller. He made a valiant effort to communicate through body language. And it worked for them. My mother seemed aware of his attempts and was pleased he was trying. And, of course, Josh translated anything important. Life might have been extremely busy, but it was working. And as if by magic the boys continued to make it to their baseball and soccer practices and games.

The lack of free time took its toll on all involved. With heightened stress there was heightened anxiety, which transferred into angry outbursts and arguments. Trevor was most susceptible, a constant reminder that life was too chaotic. But what was our alternative? I didn't dare stop the boys from their sports. This was a perfect way for them to burn off some stressful energy. As I look back, I suppose I could have searched more diligently for a new babysitter, but then I would have had to work more to pay for a hired caregiver. And the fear of Trevor's selective mutism not being understood was too great. No, our frantic schedules seemed the best option for everyone involved. And it wasn't forever. We simply needed to get through three summer months before school started again.

Amazingly we all survived that summer from hell. I honestly cannot recall much of those days. They all blurred together. What stands out most in my mind is the emotional anger—lots of anger. Trevor screamed and stomped daily, which he used as an anxiety coping method. Unfortunately, he took out most of his aggression on his brother, Josh. Not that Josh was innocent—probably far from it. After all, he was a middle schooler now and quite fluent in the art of argument. But even with the toxic environment we survived. There were no ER visits and no broken bones, only broken hearts. My husband often reminded me that the boys were rarely physical with one another. Sure, one threw the other's favorite toy and hoped it broke, but fistfights didn't happen, at least not in my presence. My husband recalled many times when his own sibling rivalries had resulted in someone bleeding and lots of black eyes. So, I counted my blessings. It could be worse. Although, the view in my mirror showed gray hair growing in a sea of brown, which confirmed the stress was taking its toll.

The school year finally approached, and the anxiety turned from anger to excitement. Although, school shopping didn't go as well as I had hoped. I can remember as a child looking forward to shopping for school supplies and new clothes (especially the new clothes). But Trevor didn't seem interested at all in shopping. Initially he resisted the idea altogether.

"Can't you go get my supplies?" he asked.

"But sweetie, don't you want to pick out a new backpack? You'll be carrying it all year, and you want to make sure you get something you like."

"Last year's backpack is fine. I can use it again."

"Um, except for this big hole in the bottom." I gestured while sliding my entire hand through the hole for emphasis.

"Oh yea, I forgot about that. Can you get me a black or orange one, then?" he asked.

"Trevor, you need to try on pants. I'm not sure what size you wear now since you've grown."

"Ok, I'll go try on pants. But can we make it quick?" He huffed in an impatient tone.

Once he got out and about, Trevor wasn't as irritable, thankfully, and began to enjoy choosing his school items. He picked out a couple of pairs of jeans and shirts along with an orange-and-black backpack. That's the Trevor I was used to, the agreeable boy who wanted to spend time with his mom. For a moment I thought he had grown up too fast and had become a teenager at age eight. Now Josh, on the other hand, was behaving like a teen at his ripe age of twelve. Something about middle school seems to turn cute little kids into evil adolescents practically overnight. I think there's an invisible force field at the school. The moment they cross over onto the other side, their personalities change, bringing out any darkness hidden prior. Fear filtered into my thoughts as I imagined the struggles this school year might bring. But why worry about something that hasn't happened yet? No, I had to remain focused on Trevor and his progress with overcoming selective mutism. He managed to speak in class last year to a couple of his friends and his teacher. Granted, he wasn't a talkative child in school, but the fact that he had used his voice was a major accomplishment. Hope reentered my mind as I prayed he combated his anxieties and spoke again.

The first day of third grade approached. Luckily, I filled out volunteer paperwork ahead of time. Trevor's new teacher, Mrs. Sundermann, was ready for me to come in during the first week of school. I thoroughly enjoyed being close to my son, even if it was only for one day.

Trevor was excited about his first day of school, especially after he found out Zach and Luke were in his class again this year. He befriended these two boys in second grade after he found his voice. So, I was hopeful the motivation would continue for him to speak in class this year. Maybe he could even initiate a conversation rather than simply replying with his quiet one- or two-word responses. But I focused on the positive: my child with selective mutism was no longer mute! Life felt normal, at least in the school setting.

Several weeks of school flew by without any major hitches. During one volunteer day as I returned to the classroom, hands full of freshly made copies, Mrs. Sundermann stopped me at her door. She guided me into the hallway, out of the children's earshot, and excitedly recalled an incident. Happy tears formed in her eyes as she shared her story.

"As you know, I allow the students to bring snacks in from home for snack time," she said. "Most of the kids bring something, but there's this little boy who never brings anything in." Her happy expression dropped to a look of concern. "I thought it was because he simply didn't want to eat anything midday, but now I realize maybe his family cannot afford it or that there may be a lack of parental support. Either way, he never shares in snack time.

"Today, he divulged to one of the students nearby that he was hungry. I overheard and replied to him, saying, 'You should have brought in a snack if you wanted to share in snack time.' He then said to me that there are no snack foods at his house to bring. My heart plunged hearing him, and I wanted to kick myself in the butt for not bringing any extra snacks. I never thought he might not have any food to bring."

The tears in her eyes threatened to spill over at any moment. As she wiped them, she continued the story. "Anyway, today was a big reminder as to why I became a teacher. Your son made the most amazing gesture, and he has reassured me there is still good in the world." The excitement returned to her facial features, and her smile grew as she spoke. "Without a single word Trevor got up to sharpen his pencil. As he walked past the little boy's desk, he slyly dropped a bag of gummies on the edge and continued walking as if nothing happened. But I saw it! I saw that kind gesture, and it brought tears to my eyes immediately! He didn't announce it to the class for attention. He did it secretly and selflessly." Now her tears streamed down her cheeks as she spoke so fondly of my child. It was at this moment I realized I shared in her tearfulness. I sniffled back the emotion, and we each took a deep breath to control our sobs.

"I always send Trevor to school with extra snacks in case he wants more," I admitted, hoping to assure her that my child had not given away his only food source.

"Whether he gave away his only snack or an extra one is irrelevant. It was the quiet gesture, the kindness, which struck me so strongly. In my thirteen years of teaching, I have never witnessed such a sweet moment. It does reassure me that I chose the right profession." Mrs. Sundermann's warm smile and bright eyes lifted my spirits, and my chest swelled with pride that I was the mother of such an amazing boy. At that moment I felt like the luckiest person in the world. Selective mutism had not stood in my child's way today; he broke free from the anxiety and reached out to help another. Sometimes his angry outbursts caused me concern for his mental health. But moments like this reassured me there was life beyond the silence, and I knew I would hold onto this memory for as long as my brain could recall memories.

CHAPTER 23

Gaining a Furry Friend

During third grade something miraculous happened. Trevor gained a best friend—not a human friend, a four-legged, furry friend. We took in a pregnant stray cat, who gave birth to five beautiful kittens. Each was unusually different. Two were orange, one long-haired and one short-haired. Trevor named them both "Crackers" since they were the color of Ritz crackers. The long-haired kitten became "Fat Crackers" since his hair puffed out like a pufferfish. There was a tiny calico who matched momma, so we called her Camo. The little white ball of fur became Marshmellow (the E being intentional since the kitten was so mellow). And the black-and-white boy reminded Trevor of the middle of the night, so he became "Midnight Stars," which described the white patches spattered over his body. We prepared Trevor for the day when the kittens would be weaned and then join their new families. But it was obvious he was attached to the little creatures. I hadn't ever seen Trevor so happy as he was when he was around those little furballs. Our adult cats didn't evoke the same excitement or interest as the kittens. Fewer arguments happened along with less stomped feet and more quietness around the house. It was a blessing, especially after the hectic summer we had. My husband and I saw the benefit of Trevor having a pet of his own, his version of an emotional support animal, so we decided he would get to choose a kitten to keep.

It was difficult for him to pick only one; he loved them all. But he bonded the most with the mellow personality of the little white ball of fur. Marshmellow became a permanent member of our family. When I saw the two together, it warmed my heart. Trevor lay on the bean bag chair and watched TV while Marshmellow licked his new master's hair. Sort of gross, but Trevor didn't mind, so I let it happen. Money could not have bought a better pet for our son. The two were inseparable.

During that school year Trevor used his voice for more than one- or two-word answers. His friends got a peek at the funny and entertaining child I've always known. And luckily my weekly volunteer days continued, so I had many opportunities to spend the entire day in Trevor's school. After one volunteer day as Trevor and I exited the building, his friend Brady tagged along toward the buses.

"I'm glad Trevor can talk now. I didn't think he knew how before last year, but he seems good at it now," Brady said. "And he's so funny, always makes me laugh. I wish he was still in my class this year."

I was charmed by Trevor's friend's admission. I glanced at Trevor, and it was obvious he was flattered by Brady's compliment. He hid his smile and pink complexion as he looked toward the buses and searched for a specific number. Then, pointing to the left, Trevor said, "There's yours, Brady. See you tomorrow!"

The two boys waved at one another, then departed happily. After we climbed into the car, my curiosity overcame my logic, and questions trickled out of my mouth before I could stop them.

"So, Brady's not in your class this year? When do you get to see him? He seems to like you, maybe we could arrange a play date?" The realization of my quizzing bombardment struck suddenly, and I felt a little nauseous at the potential reaction my son might give. I clenched my teeth together, fearful of his reaction, then awaited his reply.

"I see him in the hallway every morning when we line up before class starts. And sometimes I get to see him in the library when both of our classes go at the same time." Trevor responded calmly.

Not the worst reaction I could imagine, but I didn't want to push my luck. I told myself I would not ask him more questions. Yet, more words spilled out between my lips like a waterfall. "So, do you think he would like to come to our house for a play date? Or maybe you could get together at a restaurant or something?"

"Why is this so important to you?" Trevor asked. Slight irritation surfaced in his voice from the interrogation.

If I weren't driving the car at that moment, I would have kicked myself in the butt. Why did I have to press his buttons? I knew he was usually stressed right after school, so the last thing I should've done was grill him. But I wanted information.

"I just thought it would be fun for you to hang out with a friend now and then outside of school," I explained as I smoothed over my meddling. "And Brady seems like a nice boy."

"Yea, he's nice. But I don't want to ask him, that would be weird." He said nervously.

I considered his admission, then realized asking his friend to play might be an advanced skill he was not ready to attempt. His selective mutism showed its evil face in more than just speaking. It affected his comfort level with peer interaction as well. Social anxiety seemed to go hand in hand with selective mutism. At least, it did with my child. So, I heeded my own warning and finally closed my mouth, shutting down my inquiry. The ride home was more enjoyable after I learned to stop talking. The irony made me chuckle aloud. My child struggled to speak, and I struggled to keep quiet. If only we could meet in the middle.

Later in the school year Trevor received an invitation to Brady's birthday party at his house. I was ecstatic at the opportunity. Finally, a play date with a friend, sort of. I hoped if they had fun, Brady would invite him back or vice versa. My excitement continued to rise the closer we got to the big day. Trevor and I shopped for his friend, and he enjoyed picking out a present.

Party day arrived on a Saturday afternoon. The moment we entered the house, I heard screams from the other room. Two other boys were already present and roughhousing with one another as many boys do. The wrestling startled me, and I worried one or both might get hurt. I was lucky even though my boys were athletic, they never imitated a World Wrestling Federation match. It seemed Brady was one of the boys who held down another as a third boy counted out the pin. Finally, the boy underneath conceded his defeat and screamed, "I can't breathe!" Brady climbed off him. The smaller boy, now unpinned but flushed from the pressure, pulled himself up with the help of a nearby couch. I think we all spotted the blood that trickled down his cheek at the same time. I gasped in surprise, and Brady said in a disturbingly calm demeanor, "You're bleeding on my mom's couch."

The third boy cheerfully said, "That's awesome, you're like real worldwide wrestlers now. You're big time!"

As I glanced at Trevor, I tried to gauge his fear of the situation. But he only held a blank stare, neutral to the whole scene. I decided at that moment I would not be leaving my child at this party without my supervision. Brady's mom yelled from the other room for the boys to calm down and come eat some cake. So, the four boys and I headed for the kitchen.

After cake and punch it was time for Brady to open his presents. One of the attendees grabbed a gift and ran around the room. He held it above his head as if ready to toss it at someone at any given moment. Apparently his parental guardian either was not present among the few adults in the room or didn't notice because no one corrected the boy. Finally, Brady grabbed a package off the table and began tearing at the paper. It took everything I had to not yell at the running wild child in the room. Thankfully he realized the attention wasn't on him any longer and stopped. Joining the rest of us around the birthday boy, he managed to contain his restlessness long enough for all the presents to be opened. Well, almost. As soon as Brady opened the next-to-last present, a transformer, the boy grabbed it, slung it under his arm like a football, and sprinted away from the group. Brady sprang up from his spot and chased the other boy, leaving the last present unopened on the table. The third boy joined the other two as they ran from room to room, tossing the transformer back and forth in an impromptu game of keep-away. Trevor got up slowly, walked to the edge of the room, and watched the high-intensity activity from a safe distance. I glanced at the mom in charge and waited for her to control this madhouse behavior. Instead, she got up and asked another mother if she'd like a glass of wine. What? At a child's party? I supposed that was one way of handling all the chaos: tune it out by numbing your brain. My face must have revealed my shock because she then asked me if I would like some wine too. Obviously she misinterpreted my expression as surprise for being left out of the wine invite. Well, yes I would enjoy the temporary escape, but it simply didn't feel like the appropriate time to indulge, so I declined. I did, however, ask about the remaining unopened gift and was told it was something Brady's aunt had gotten him, so he could open it later. I deduced the hyperactivity must be a familiar experience in this home, given the indifference. At that moment Trevor gathered enough courage and dashed across the floor toward the fallen transformer toy. My stomach plunged in fear as he reached out to scoop it up. I worried my child would be flattened at the bottom of an inevitable boy pileup. Luckily, one of the other children beat him to it and dashed away. A pileup still occurred, but fortunately Trevor was not involved and slithered to the other side of the room, away from the rowdy boys. Screaming kids could be heard a mile away, I was sure. Or maybe my own head echoed from the reverberated sounds and amplified it to sound louder. Either way, my head pounded and told me I had had enough. After I thanked the parent in charge (or so-called), I called for Trevor to say his goodbyes. Amazingly, he obliged without any fuss, which led me to believe maybe he, too, was overstimulated by the energetic play.

In the car Trevor was still wound up by the excitement of the party and chatted nearly nonstop the whole drive home. The moment we pulled into our driveway, he jumped out of the car and ran for the house. He darted through the kitchen and into the living room. I immediately yelled at him, "STOP RUNNING IN THE HOUSE!" Unfortunately, I couldn't stop my mouth from the follow-up jab. "THIS IS NOT BRADY'S HOUSE, WE DON'T ACT LIKE THAT HERE!"

Trevor slowed down to a light jog as he continued through the house and down the hallway, searching for his brother to share his adventures. Within a few minutes I heard familiar screams from their bedroom. Time for an intervention. My footfall on the wooden hall floor gave enough warning for the boys of my arrival. By the time I reached their room, they were playing contentedly on opposite sides and looked up at me with their best attempt at innocence. I shook my head and could only imagine what had happened only moments before I stepped into that doorway. But for now they settled themselves, and it was good enough for me. Time for a glass of wine. The silent thought made me smile. Both boys took my expression as a win, and they smiled too.

The remainder of third grade was calmer than the party, but our home life became more stressful. Trevor's anger issues rose, and I was unsure how to help him. We separated the boys and gave each their own room. It seemed time since Josh was becoming a teenager. It became a common occurrence to hear Trevor yell, stomp down the hallway, and slam his door. After a few minutes passed, I would hear him open his door enough to let in Marshmellow, and then both would disappear into his room again. Time with his fur friend always helped calm Trevor down, but it didn't prevent his anger from striking in the first place.

My husband, ex-husband, and I struggled with our staggered schedules to cover our babysitting needs yet again over the summer before fourth grade. We had survived the previous summer, so we figured we were experts now and our victory could be repeated. I also reduced my work schedule to a bare minimum, making only enough money for the necessities. The time I spent with my children was more valuable than money—at least, that's what I told myself as I trudged forward in our current situation. Stress became our norm. It was not a question of whether the boys would get along. The question was, when will they start arguing? This highly strained lifestyle was also affecting the adults involved, and tempers flared nearly daily. Fortunately, my husband and I knew this was temporary, and eventually we would come out on the other side. Each day that passed got us closer to the next school year and shifting back to our regular schedules. We made it through the high-intensity summer days. We were not entirely unscathed, but finally fourth grade arrived!

CHAPTER 24

Running for Student Council

Trevor adjusted to his new role as a "normal" child during fourth grade. He continued using his voice with a few friends and consistently answered any questions directed his way by the teacher. But he still struggled to voluntarily participate in class. He wouldn't raise his hand to offer answers ever. His fourth grade teacher wasn't only new to him but also the profession. We determined this was a good thing for us since she was still enthusiastic about her job. She was energetic and ready for anything these elementary schoolers threw her way.

One day, Trevor came home from school more excited than usual.

"I need help making a poster for school. Some of the kids want me to run for student council." His words surprised me, and I gave him a blank look for several moments. "Will you help me?" he asked, confused by my quietness.

"Oh, yes, of course." I finally managed to reply with feigned enthusiasm. "Did you have something in mind?" Bewilderment over this topic still swirled in my head while I awaited his answer.

"No, just a poster that says to vote for me."

"Is this something you *want* to do, Trevor? Or are you only doing it to make your friends happy?" I asked as I still struggled to comprehend this whole unfamiliar, volunteering-to-participate-in-something concept.

"I want to do it, but my friends did nominate me. They think I would be good at it, and my teacher agrees. And I don't really have to do much if I get elected except go to meetings and stuff," he explained casually.

Who was this boy?

"And I might not even get elected," he continued, preparing himself as much as me for this disappointing possibility. "But I think I have a good chance. There are only five running in my class, and they usually pick two or three."

As my brain wrapped around the idea, I began to love the thought of Trevor being the center of attention for once. Could he handle being in the spotlight? At home he loved attention, thrived on making us laugh. But in public he was a different Trevor. He was a selectively mute version of himself: a timid, quiet, shy child. Maybe it was time the world got to know the real him. My face broke into a genuine smile as my eyes lit up in anticipation of the idea.

"Yes, I can help you make the best poster ever!" I confidently announced. Then, we began brainstorming ideas on how to create this best poster ever.

After I suggested Trevor use a photo of himself for his poster, he decided on one of him with his cat, Marshmellow. I used Photoshop to edit the photo and changed Marshmellow into a tiger, hopeful the true essence of his bravery was displayed. If Trevor's happy smile and bright eyes or the bravery of having posed with a "live tiger" weren't enough to win over his subjects, then the slogan we came up with surely would. "If you're clever, then vote for Trevor!" What fourth grader could pass up an opportunity to be clever? After several posters were printed out, Trevor worked on his speech.

I only offered guidance on the layout of the speech, which gave Trevor the freedom to write what he wanted to say. After all, this was his speech, not mine. It needed to be written in his words. I might be a little partial to my son (ok, a lot), but I believe he wrote the best fourth grade student council speech ever. I would have voted for him for all available student council spots. But I doubt anyone would have believed I was a fourth grader, so my voting option remained a dream. And worse than not having a vote, I wouldn't get to hear my son read his speech. If only I was a fly on the classroom wall during speech time. This idea triggered a thought that maybe if I conveniently dropped by the classroom at precisely the time the speeches were read, I could listen through the door while Trevor won over the children. After I shook the craziness out of my head, I promised myself I would not overstep my motherly obligation. I did not want a new title of "smother" or "helicopter mom." I remained a normal, supportive mother on the sidelines and waited for my child to tell me all the details.

As I listened to him do a read-through of his speech, it brought on a mixture of emotions. Feelings of excitement, humor, and pride in my son forged tears of joy in my eyes as he read aloud his persuasive words:

> "For those of you who don't know me, my name is Trevor.
> For those of you who do know me, my name is Trevor.
> And as my sign says, 'if you're clever, then vote for Trevor!'"
> Since I'm the only Trevor in this class, that means vote for me.
> As a student council representative, I will work hard and raise money for our school.
> I'm willing to give up my own recess time to be in student council.
> Be clever and vote for Trevor, and I will do my very best as your student council representative."

After he read, I couldn't stop the overflow of emotion as tears trickled down my cheeks. He was going to win over anyone who could hear his words. Then, butterflies suddenly fluttered in my stomach at the thought of Trevor getting stage fright and not being able to speak aloud on speech day. What if he didn't have enough courage and was unable to read his words to his class? Instead of dwelling on my own fears, I swallowed down a gulp of air, then forced a supportive smile. He could do this! I had to have faith in my child. And if he genuinely wanted to do this, then he would do it.

The next couple of weeks leading up to election day seemed to fly by. Trevor didn't seem nervous the morning of speech day, but twice he checked that he had his speech in his backpack on the ride to school.

"Will the speeches be read first thing in the morning?" I asked curiously.

"No, but sometime before lunch. My teacher said there are a couple of things we have to do first, and then we'll do the speeches," he explained.

Well, so much for nonchalantly arriving at the perfect time to hear his speech being read. I knew I couldn't do it, although the thought still lingered.

Once we arrived at school, I kissed Trevor's head briefly and wished him luck with his speech, and he climbed out of the car with a quick "I love you" sign exchange. I watched him as he walked through the doors of the building. I then said a little prayer that he would find the strength and courage to speak in front of his class.

All through my workday my thoughts drifted to Trevor reading his speech. I was positive the kids would love it and also positive he would be elected by his classmates. But the fear of the expected positive outcome made me nervous. I distracted myself from the straying thoughts and tried not to assume the results. Finally, the clock ticked, and time was up. School was over.

I raced to the bus stop after work, which was a common practice. It seemed I could never get my home care patients to stop talking so I could leave on time. (Ok, maybe I was partly to blame.) The moment I was within visual range, I saw the bus as it turned the corner at the other end of the road. My foot pressed the accelerator a little faster since I knew my son was already dropped off and would have news of the day. The car sped down the road and went slightly airborne after hitting a bump, which gave me a boost of adrenaline and increased my excitement. "Woohoo!" I heard myself scream, then realized I must have looked like a crazy person when I shouted aloud alone in the car. Fortunately, not a soul passed me at that moment to witness my craziness.

I pulled up in front of the house, and Trevor came running out immediately. His face displayed excitement.

"Well, how'd you do today?" I asked timidly, hopeful his happy expression was about the day and not the fact that I was home and could do a McDonald's run for him.

"Great! I was voted in for student council," he announced joyfully.

"*What?* That's awesome!" I replied, truly overjoyed by the news. "So, the kids liked your speech?"

"Yes, they laughed at my joke." He answered with a grin plastered from ear to ear.

"I knew they would love it! You did a fantastic job, sweetie. I'm proud of you."

"Proud enough to get chicken nuggets at McDonald's?" he asked. The devious sparkle in his eyes and the smug look made me laugh. He knew darn well I couldn't resist him. And his victory was worthy of celebration. Looked like we were having McDonald's for dinner (again).

CHAPTER 25

Benefits of Animal Therapy

Trevor attended his weekly student council meetings, collected aluminum tab tops from pop cans for a fundraiser, and gained friends during fourth grade. His selective mutism did not get in his way of conversing in public, but his anger issues continued at home. He and his brother fought often. Yelling wars were a common occurrence nearly the minute they got home. We signed up Trevor to see a counselor for his anger issues. The visits helped a little, but the stress of getting him to the office promptly created its own problems. The whole family often yelled at one another, and it was not a fun household. We finally decided the added stress of the counselor appointments outweighed the benefits received, so we stopped taking him. Trevor learned to use deep breathing as a calming technique, but his cat offered the most effective support, and the added benefit of reduced stress from not having set appointments to attend reduced Trevor's outbursts.

The impending summer posed a new obstacle for us. Josh joined the marching band and had all-day practices during the two weeks of band camp. This left Trevor by himself. After some discussion with Trevor about what he might be interested in doing during Josh's stint away, he decided horse camp would be fun. So, we enrolled him in a two-week horse day camp. Trevor couldn't wait for fourth grade to be over and counted the days until horse camp. He drew and molded horses out of playdough during his free time.

During the couple of weekends leading up to Trevor's big event, we visited my sister-in-law in the country. Trevor practiced riding with the horses at her farm, and my husband enjoyed teaching the boys how to look like authentic cowboys. The sight of the three of them with grass stems hanging out of their mouths was priceless. Trevor's little nose wrinkled up in disgust at first as he expected it to taste bad. But then he realized there wasn't much flavor, so he embraced the chance to look like a cowboy. He even got bucked off Cricket once while he rode. Well, not actually bucked off per se, but he slid to the ground, so Nick declared Trevor a real cowboy after that incident. I was worried he would develop a fear of horses after he fell off one, but he "got back up on that horse" with newly found courage. His excitement about horse camp increased after the weekends at his aunt's farm.

Fortunately, time flew from all the fun, and the first week of horse camp finally arrived. As we pulled up to the horse stables, I spotted three other kids at the picnic tables awaiting their first training class. One of the girls had on black rain boots, and the other two kids wore athletic shoes like Trevor. It's funny how insignificant details get stuck in your brain. We joined them at the picnic tables, and then their camp counselor arrived. There was an energy in the air from all the excitement, and I shared in their emotion. A big part of me wanted to join the class, too, especially after I peeked into the barn and glimpsed a few horses. The beautiful, long-nosed creatures neighed to be petted, reminding me of my youth when I lived in the country and rode our neighbor's horses. Unfortunately, I was four when we moved to the city, so my horse experience was limited. After the next two weeks Trevor's horse knowledge would far surpass mine. I couldn't wait to hear his stories.

After the first day of horse camp, I returned promptly to pick up Trevor. He ran out to the car and smiled ear to ear. Right away he filled me in on the highlights of the day.

"My horse is named Rudy and is really cool. He's mostly brown, but he also has some white on him. I think he likes me. I like him." As he rambled a bit about meeting his horse, I probed further for specific details.

"So, what was the class like this morning?"

"Oh, we just learned the names of the stuff we have to use to take care of our horses. I couldn't believe there were so many things. Did you know that horses' hooves keep growing, so you have to file them down?" The light in his eyes revealed the excitement in his heart, and I knew this was going to be a fantastic learning experience for my son. But I did want to know one more important detail.

"Did you talk to any new friends today? Have anything in common with anyone?" I asked with less emphasis on the harsh word *talk*.

"There was only one other boy there, and he's older than me. But he seems nice," Trevor answered, managing to avoid my underlying question.

I stopped questioning him and listened as he rambled on about meeting his horse. Unfortunately, visitors were not allowed to attend horse camp with the children. Only the paid attendees sat in on the classes. So, my presence was limited to pickup times. Once, I managed to snap a photo of Trevor standing next to Rudy in the stable, but I never got to witness him riding. Trevor didn't seem to mind. In fact, he was a little relieved I couldn't watch over him and snap a ton of pictures throughout the day. Sometimes it was difficult to know how involved my child needed me to be to help him deal with his anxieties, and the rules seemed to change from day to day. One time he wanted me there, then the next he didn't. It fluctuated with his mood, and I supposed I was like that too. Some days I felt mentally stronger than others. It made sense when I considered his anxiety in that manner.

The last day of horse camp brought on a slew of emotions. I expected Trevor to be sad about saying goodbye to Rudy, so I brought him McDonald's chicken nuggets to help lift his spirits when I picked him up.

Trevor waved briefly to the other kids, then trotted quickly to our car. He was ready to go—that confused me. I expected he would want to hang out longer and stretch out camp time. But no, he was ready.

"What's going on, didn't you have a good day at camp today?" I asked, puzzled by his body language.

"Yea, it was fun," he answered, but his sentence hung out there in the air for a moment before he continued his explanation. "But we had to do a play today. I thought it was stupid."

"A play? Was it about horses?" I asked encouragingly.

"No, it was about cops and robbers," he replied. The frustration was apparent in his voice. "I would have rather ridden Rudy longer than do a stupid play."

"Oh, cops and robbers, huh? That's kind of weird. Maybe if it had been about cowboys and Indians, that might have made more sense," I said, siding with my son. "What part did you play?" I asked, secretly excited about Trevor acting out a play with other children and using his voice aloud.

"I was a cop. I didn't really have any lines, I just stood there like a guard. It was kinda boring," he replied, not impressed by the turn of events.

Eventually he gave enough information that I deduced his regular camp instructor left early for an appointment, so someone else filled in. Since it was so late in the day, they did filler activities until the kids were picked up. I didn't admit to Trevor that I felt this interactive time was beneficial because he wasn't in the best mood to handle disagreement. He was going to miss Rudy, and his emotions were challenging him at that moment. Instead, I let him eat his snack while we listened to music on the ride home. I believe this horse camp was one of the best decisions we made to that point in the recovery of his anxieties. He didn't have any meltdowns during that two-week phase and seemed much calmer and together. I prayed for lasting results, but deep down I knew it was only a matter of time before his anger resurfaced.

CHAPTER 26

Trevor's Veterans Day Speech

Fifth grade brought on a whole new set of issues. While Trevor was among the older kids in his school, he also had to prepare himself for the upcoming change. Middle school was right around the corner, and for a child with anxieties that's a big deal. Trevor had his first male teacher that year, and surprisingly I knew him from my school-age days. So, Trevor's bond was nearly instantaneous with the man. He had a positive fifth grade experience and enjoyed his teacher and made new friends. But he still came home agitated, frustrated, and angry, especially with his brother. The two struggled to get along and only managed a few calm minutes together before the yelling began. This led to screaming matches, in which they both won. Life was a constant argument. We bought video games, which worked temporarily for controlling the angry outbursts—that is, until Trevor lost or anticipated he was about to lose. Trevor did not handle failure well. He needed an outlet for his anxiety, but video games were not the answer.

The school year passed quickly, probably too quickly for comfort from Trevor's perspective. In preparation for the sixth grade band, there was an instrument tryout one evening, which Trevor attended. Since Josh played trumpet in the band, Trevor had his heart set on playing anything other than the same instrument. He and Josh argued enough at home, so the last thing he wanted to do was follow in his brother's footsteps.

On the evening of music tryouts, there were volunteers in various parts of the band room, office, and hallway. They each gave a brief explanation about their specific instrument to a handful of fifth graders. Each child was given a chance to choose an instrument for trial. They were scored according to their ability to play said instrument.

Trevor avoided the trumpet area and immediately visited the trombone section. He was handed a clean mouthpiece by the band director and asked to blow into it. Amazingly, a sound came out. Not a pretty sound, but more than just air—almost a duck call (or a dying duck). I was impressed, as was the band director. He then attached the mouthpiece to a trombone and instructed Trevor how to hold it. Again, he made a sound. This time the sound was a low, raspy rumble. Apparently that wasn't a bad first attempt, and he recommended Trevor consider choosing trombone to play in sixth grade band. The paper he handed him displayed a score of five out of five under the trombone section. But he encouraged him to try more instruments before he made his final decision.

Somehow Trevor got swept into a group of students headed for the next station. He didn't fight the crowd but walked along with them. He soon discovered he was face to face with the trumpet instructor. Trevor had been curious as to how Josh played the trumpet, so he decided to try.

The instructor handed Trevor a clean mouthpiece and listened as he blew into it. The sound was strong. He then handed him a trumpet to attach to the mouthpiece. Trevor blew again, and another strong sound came out through the bell. With a twinkle of excitement in his eye, the instructor showed Trevor how to place his fingers on the finger buttons and play a note. A sweet musical noise bellowed into the air. Even though I knew nothing about musical instruments, I knew it sounded good.

The trumpet instructor spent several more minutes with Trevor and showed him different notes. Each time his face lit up more and more as Trevor played the sounds correctly. It was indisputable: he was a natural. Finally, the trumpet instructor handed Trevor the scoring paper for his audition, displaying a bold circle around the number five. As Trevor reached for the paper, the instructor said, "I highly, highly, highly recommend you choose trumpet as your instrument for next year."

Trevor's face lit up in response to the compliment, and he couldn't stop smiling. It was in that moment I knew both of my boys would be trumpet players.

At home I eased into telling Josh the news that Trevor was going to play the same instrument as he did in band next year. I expected the worst, but Josh surprised me with his cooperativeness. Instead, he seemed excited that Trevor had chosen the trumpet, flattered almost. Hope rose in my chest. Maybe this was the common bond they needed to foster a better brotherly relationship. Time would tell.

At the beginning of May the fifth graders were assigned an essay to write about veterans in honor of the upcoming Military Appreciation Day. Trevor's essay was heartfelt and full of respect for our soldiers. Since I am the type of person who cries while the national anthem plays, I was especially proud that he displayed such respect and love for his country. When he came home with the news that his essay was chosen to be read in front of the entire school at an upcoming assembly, I was elated.

"Oh my gosh, that's wonderful news!" I exclaimed. "Who will be reading the chosen essays?"

"We each read our own," Trevor answered matter-of-factly.

"Really? In front of the whole school?" Oops, I accidentally said my fearful thoughts aloud. That was the last thing my son needed to hear, but it was too late. My comments could not be unheard.

"I could have someone read mine for me if I really want, but everyone else is going to read theirs themselves, so I'd feel kinda funny if I didn't do it too," he explained as worry lines took shape on his face.

I attempted to reassure him and said, "Oh, I'm sure it won't be that bad since everyone will be reading their speeches."

As I smiled at my anxious son, I silently regretted having planted more fear in his mind. How could he ever overcome his anxieties if I continually emphasized the negatives?

Soon enough, assembly day arrived. Luckily, the parents were invited, so I arranged my workday to allow plenty of time for the event. There was no way I wanted to miss such an important moment in Trevor's life.

As I climbed toward the top row of the audience stands in the gymnasium, I glanced around and was pleased by the plentiful attendance. The top row made it slightly challenging to see details from such a distance, but it provided adequate back support if one leaned against the wall. And Trevor was familiar with this chosen location, so he knew where to glance to find me.

The students entered the gymnasium, led by their corresponding teachers. I watched the children as they waddle behind the adults, and the scene gave me an urge to quack like a duck. Fortunately, I managed to contain the urge to a low whisper. Luckily, no one was in earshot, so my immaturity went unheard. I spotted my child at the rear of a line of students from his class. He glanced upward toward the wall and scanned the top row until our eyes met. We shared a quick smile, and then his eyes darted downward in slight embarrassment as he continued on to take a seat on the floor where his teacher indicated. After all the kids were guided into rows on the floor in front of the audience stands, the principal entered.

Once she reached the podium, the speakers squeaked as the principal spoke into the microphone. The entire body was directed into standing, and we recited the Pledge of Allegiance. After we took our seats once again, the principal then introduced a lieutenant colonel officer, who took center stage. He spoke to the children about Armistice Day being celebrated at the end of WWI and how it is now called Veterans Day. He spoke about how Military Appreciation Day was begun to honor current military personnel and explained the reason for today's event. As he passed the mic back to the principal, it was time for the chosen essays to be read. She called up four children, two from each fifth grade class. Each child stood and walked to the front next to the podium after they heard their name. Trevor looked nervous as he stood in front of the whole school. He held his paper with both hands, and his eyes were locked on the ground. The children next to him didn't look much calmer as they fidgeted in place, appearing to dance to an unheard song. (Or maybe it was the "need to potty" dance.) After the first two speeches were read, it was Trevor's turn.

The principal held the microphone near Trevor's face while he read his speech aloud. My heart soared at the sound of his sweet voice echoing throughout the gymnasium. He did it. He spoke in public. Trevor focused on his paper and followed word for word. He never looked up. He finished his speech in less than a minute, but time seemed frozen in my mind while he was the center of attention. When the principal moved to the last child, I exhaled a breath I hadn't known I was holding. Then, a tear dropped to my cheek. My baby, my selective mutism-struggling child, overcame the intense anxiety and used his voice in front of others—many, many others. I could not have been prouder of his accomplishment. After the final child read their essay, the crowd clapped in response. I screamed out cheerfully as I clapped and whistled. (And by "whistle" I mean loudly yelled "woohoo" since I lacked the skill to make a true whistle sound.) A few nearby parents noticed my extreme response and gave me awkward looks. But my excitement did not waver. I wanted to make sure every single person heard my appreciation for the bravery of those children who read to us, especially my son. The officer shook each of their hands and thanked them for their speeches.

I am not sure if that moment was stored in the long-term memory of the other three children who read their essays that day, but my son never forgot it—although his recollection may not include a lunatic mother who shouted from the top bench of the stands. But the emotion of the day would never be forgotten. Fifth grade was a turning point in his life.

CHAPTER 27

Saying Goodbye to Grandma

Earlier that summer we got the horrible news that Trevor's grandmother was diagnosed with terminal lung cancer. Normal life stopped. (As if life was ever normal!) We catered to my mother while Trevor's issues were pushed to the back burner. After she became quite ill from chemotherapy, we decided she needed a break from the damaging treatments to enjoy living. So, we rented a conversion van and headed to Florida for some fun in the sun.

It was astounding how wonderful a caregiver Trevor became. He probably always had these tendencies in him, but we never had the opportunity to witness it before this situation. My mother picked up on his willingness and began to rely on him the most of the four of us. Trevor was next to her nearly the whole vacation and ensured she safely negotiated the steps to the van. He often asked her if she needed to sit and rest and offered to fetch any necessary items. He couldn't have found his voice at a better time! He finally spoke to his grandmother. We were all proud of him. Fortunately, my mother's health improved after our two-week trip, so we then could shift our focus temporarily to the boys and their upcoming school year.

Sixth grade was a smoother transition than I feared. It seemed change was easier for Trevor to handle than expected. We always thought he thrived on a set routine, but the opposite was also true. Being at a different school and around people who were unaware of his silent past gave him the courage to use his voice more. He was given a second chance to be a normal kid among his peers. Middle school went well for Trevor, at least for overcoming his verbal issue. At home his anger outbursts continued, but we assumed some of this was a natural part of the tween years as his hormones guided him more than his anxiety. But not all his fury could be attributed to his age. I believe when it came to Trevor, we turned a blind eye to his outbursts and allowed him more freedom. In light of my mother's medical status, we overlooked attitudes from either son. Maybe I was numb to life and overly worried about my mother, so I didn't react when they lashed out. With the terminal diagnosis the entire family went through a grieving period as if we had already lost her. Sometimes we were exceptionally nice to one another. Then, as if a light switched on, we were the complete opposite and yelled about trivial issues. None of the family was immune. We all fought, but we bounced back quickly, and the boys seemed more sensitive and sincere. They often apologized without any needed intervention—or maybe my husband talked to them when I didn't notice.

The final month my mother spent in the hospital as she battled her disease was the biggest strain on our family. I wanted to be with her every waking hour, but logistically this didn't work. A typical day began with the boys being dropped off at school, and then I drove to the hospital to visit mom. After school hours my husband brought the boys to hospice to see both of us. We shared many dinners in the family lounge area. Nick took the boys home after visiting hours so they could do their homework. Often Trevor and Josh were already asleep by the time I arrived home. But I popped into their rooms and whispered "I love you" to my sons as they slept. It was the most challenging month of my entire life. I felt torn between my own mother and my children. But my husband was such an awesome support throughout the ordeal and often reassured me the boys would still be there after my mother wasn't.

April Fool's Day arrived along with the news my mother had passed. The day fit her humorous personality. Her battle had ended, and it was time to pick up the pieces. As we learned to live again, we struggled through the difficult time as a stronger family. It brought out the best and worst of Trevor. He cooperated more but not until after he had an anger-induced meltdown. While everyone in our household struggled to control their emotions, Trevor's defiance escalated. Fortunately for me, I was still numb for several months after our family loss, so this parental burden passed to my husband. He was typically calm and had a high tolerance for irritations. He handled the whole situation well, but in the end his fuse grew short too. I think the anger was contagious.

We bought Trevor a punching bag as a healthier outlet for his anger, and it worked. Eventually our lives began to feel normal again (or whatever that meant in our case). Trevor's anger subsided along with our household stress levels. I'm still unsure which came first, the chicken or the egg—Trevor being the chicken and stress the egg—but it became obvious that his increased anger was directly related to the higher stress levels. So, reducing stress was the best approach to controlling his anxiety. We embraced this low-stress lifestyle concept.

Like most good plans ours started strong with high motivation. But soon none of us followed the plan as it fizzled into nonexistence. Josh's high school years added substantial stress, which he often released in Trevor's direction. We kept the two apart whenever possible, and this tactic decreased stress at home until Josh became a licensed driver. Like many families we latched onto this new asset and bartered with automobile time. Josh was loaned the car keys when he drove his brother around. While this helped tremendously with our parental stress, it wasn't the best option for our boys. They were arguing the moment they entered our house. After throwing down their belongings, they stormed off to their separate rooms. But having them ride together made financial sense. It offered more time for me to work and saved on gas. If they were going to the same place at the same time, they rode together.

Trevor excelled in band and practiced his trumpet regularly. He earned first chair throughout middle school, which was a huge accomplishment. His success helped reduce his anger issues and gave him another method for controlling his outbursts. After we realized the positive influence music had on our child, we hired a private instructor and encouraged Trevor's new passion. The one-on-one sessions were perfect for his selective mutism and allowed Trevor the comfort of using his voice when needed in a nonthreatening environment. His love of music continued, and miraculously he also started to get along better with his brother.

Summers were easier with teenagers. For the most part they were self-sufficient. I hired my sister to drop in midday to ensure they ate a real lunch so potato chips weren't being relied on for their sustenance. Often Trevor had already made lunch for Josh and himself, usually ramen noodles or spaghetti. But we were reassured by having an adult drop in and monitor them. I believe since the boys knew their Aunt Sharon came by daily, it encouraged better behavior. Neither wanted her to see misbehavior, so they were perfect little angels . . .

. . . Until she left. Then, the text messaging war began as each complained about the other. I usually found it comical until their disagreements escalated into phone calls interrupting my work. Thankfully, this was infrequent. I felt lucky to have such great boys.

Trevor became a familiar face with the marching band throughout Josh's high school years. He helped us "pit crew" parents load the equipment on and off the field and trucks. Trevor even earned his own pit crew shirt with his name embroidered on it. Although he didn't initiate speaking during those days, he would answer questions directed his way.

Every marching band season the director asked Trevor, "How many years before you'll be in high school so you can join the marching band?" It became our countdown until Trevor's own marching band experience. With the boys four grades apart, they were separated in school. I felt sad they missed out on extracurricular activities together. During the marching band season there was an eighth grade night. During one home football game at halftime, the eighth grade band members were invited to play alongside the marching band. This coming season was our year for the boys to play together on the field. It made a perfect photo opportunity, both boys side by side as they played their trumpets. I even had a new camera with a zoom lens. I was so ready!

The summer before Josh's senior year, Trevor attended the parent meeting with me on the first day of Josh's band camp. Rumor had it the band director picked one eighth grader to trial in the marching band, so we both wanted to be there to hear the details. Excitement buzzed through us in anticipation that Trevor might have been the one picked. Before the start of the meeting, whispers identified the needed instrument as a baritone. I knew a baritone wasn't a trumpet, so my hopes for Trevor to be the "chosen one" dwindled fast. During the parent meeting the band director confirmed it was a baritone spot he needed to fill and explained to us that all would be revealed later after he spoke to the chosen eighth grader. He emphasized that they needed to be mature and responsible. Doubt clouded my mind, but I knew we always had eighth grade night for my two boys to stand together and play.

After the parent meeting Trevor and I headed down the hallway of the school to leave. I heard the band director as he called Trevor's name. He jogged toward us through the crowd, then immediately asked Trevor, "Would you be willing to march this season, and if so, can you stay for band camp today?"

"Yes!" The word tumbled out of Trevor's mouth hastily as if he feared the opportunity would disappear if he delayed his answer.

"What?" I asked, slightly confused. "I thought you needed a baritone player."

"We do, but I have no doubt Trevor can learn it. The fingering is the same." And with that brief explanation the band director placed his arm on Trevor's shoulder and guided him out the door toward the practice field. I stood in awe as I watched my baby grow up before my eyes.

CHAPTER 28

From Struggler to Leader

With both of my boys at band camp, I spent most of my free time watching from the sidelines. Trevor's new baritone was much bigger than his trumpet. I feared he couldn't hold it up for an entire ten-minute show. He looked so small among the other students, but he was the youngest after all. In the beginning they had Trevor separated and receiving one-on-one training as he learned to march. But he quickly picked up the technique and joined into the larger mob. Throughout the day they divided into smaller groups with their corresponding instruments and practiced the music. I expected Trevor to struggle with the baritone, but I was mistaken. He blended in as if he had always played it.

Throughout band camp practices I rarely saw Trevor talk to any of the other students. This sparked fear. I wondered if he was being pushed too quickly into the marching band and if it would cause his SM issues to resurface. But then, as I looked closer at the situation, I saw that the kids didn't have much time to chat with their lengthy twelve-hour practices. But Trevor still tried to find his place within the group. He came home at night smiling and happy along with being exhausted from the vigorous activity. I decided he was mature enough, and he handled the added responsibilities well.

Trevor entered the school year with new confidence. As the only eighth grade member in the marching band, it helped him feel stronger and more self-assured. He lived up to the band director's expectations for maturity, which also helped control his anxiety. My fears of his new marching band role subsided. He found his own path. During the end-of-band-camp party, Trevor was showered with attention and awards from fellow low brass members. He made friends and fit in regardless of his anxiety issues.

During the marching band season, eighth grade night approached. I had already had several opportunities to see my boys march together on the field, but they weren't next to one another since they played different instruments. Eight grade night was special because they played the same instrument for the first time. I'm not sure which son was prouder, Trevor or his big brother, Josh. They stood side by side at the front of the trumpet line and played their hearts out that night. It was a memorable moment for us all and marked the beginning of a new phase in our lives. I cherished the family bonding time marching band provided. My husband and I attended every football game and band competition. We worked behind the scenes with the equipment, which gave us a front-row view of the boys. While they didn't necessarily hang out together, they were always within earshot of one another. And since I was the unofficial band photographer, I captured a ton of photos of each without invading their social lives. All the band kids loved the photos I posted throughout the season, especially the silly action shots the official photographer wasn't around to capture. Life was full and fun.

For our last combined spring break vacation, we decided to reenact our first trip. After we explored caves and zip lined in Kentucky, we made our final stop at the park we had first visited eleven years prior. The boys cooperated amazingly well and rushed to the playground equipment to take their places for the perfect photo comparison. Fortunately, it was close to dusk and chilly, so no one else visited the park during our escapade. The before and after photos we captured will be cherished for a lifetime.

Once Josh graduated and moved away to college, Trevor became our only child at home. The first spring break neared. The boys' school break schedules were different, and we were unsure how to proceed with traditional vacations. After a family meeting we discussed our options and decided to continue the mother-son bonding time until Trevor graduated high school. Since Josh couldn't be there in person, I created a "Josh-on-a-stick" with a photo of his face on cardboard taped to a stick. Trevor and I took Josh-on-a-Stick everywhere we visited during our week touring Chicago together.

One day while we walked along the water's edge in the windy city, we spotted three young ladies who looked to be about the same age as Josh. An idea popped into my head. I wanted a photo of Josh-on-a-Stick with the girls for spring break. After I shared this thought with Trevor, he immediately responded, "You're not really going to ask them to take their picture, are you?"

"Well yea, why not?" I responded, surprised he didn't share in the excitement of such a brilliant idea.

"Then you're doing it alone," he stated matter-of-factly.

So, off I headed alone toward the three girls. They sat on the edge of a wooden dock. As I glanced back to watch Trevor's reaction, I discovered he was nowhere to be found. Had I embarrassed my child? After I explained the whole situation about why I carried a young man's face on a stick, the girls were delighted to help in my quest for a spring break photo with him. Although, with the missing son nowhere in sight, the girls shared a few sideways glances as they questioned the validity of my story. Whether they believed me or not, I got the photo I desired. And when I walked far enough away from the girls, Trevor reappeared from behind a tree. I blamed it on his selective mutism once again showing its ugly face. But then again, maybe he was reacting the way any teenage boy would in the presence of three girls and one crazy mom.

When Josh attended our previous annual spring break trips, we had the perfect bonding opportunity for the three of us. But these trips didn't provide Trevor with many opportunities for interaction with others. As I think about each of the years we took a trip, I realize there were only a handful of times when Trevor was in a position to use his voice with outsiders. Maybe this was a blessing in disguise and gave him time to develop comfort in public situations without the stress. Now the trips were only the two of us (and Josh-on-a-Stick), so Trevor was more compelled to use his voice. He didn't have his big brother to speak for him, and there was no other child to distract attention. It was only Trevor. Every restaurant opportunity allowed Trevor to speak when he ordered his food. And when we visited touristy areas, people often reached out to us. They would ask where we were from and broach other topics of small talk. Apparently a mother-son duo was more approachable than a family of three. Or maybe it was because we carried around a stick person. Whatever the reason, Trevor used his voice more, and I felt like he was finally cured—as if there was such a thing.

Trevor caught onto the fact that people talked to him more when he carried Josh-on-a-Stick, so he began to carry his brother less. He wasn't totally against me carrying him in public, but he was happier when we left him seat-belted in the car.

Toward the end of Trevor's junior year in high school, he informed me of his plans to try out for the drum major position in the marching band. This was a big deal. If he made it for one of the three positions they chose, he would be leading over two hundred kids. Granted, most of the time that "leading" would involve waving his arms in time with the music and directing the musicians while they played their instruments and marched on the field in their formations. But every practice would include shouting commands and giving pep talks as needed. It was a huge deal, and I was shocked Trevor would consider doing it. For having a social anxiety disorder, my son sure did put himself into challenging positions.

I considered approaching the band director about Trevor's selective mutism. I hoped it might persuade him to choose Trevor for drum major if he knew about the disability. But it occurred to me that the opposite might also happen: he might intentionally not choose him if he suspected he couldn't handle the pressure. My husband and I discussed the options and finally decided it would be best not to say a word. If Trevor was chosen, it would be completely on his own merit with no outside help. That was the fairest choice.

Trevor turned in his application and requested to be considered for tryouts. Nine contenders were approved and ready to compete for the three open positions. The month-long ordeal included workshops that taught each participant how to properly conduct and offered leadership tutoring classes. No matter the outcome, I knew this experience would be rewarding and beneficial for all involved, especially Trevor. He seemed so excited and committed to the band, and his enthusiasm was contagious to all around him.

The day finally arrived for the conclusion of tryouts. Most of the band members volunteered to be in the tryout band. Each competing participant had their chance to lead the band in two familiar songs. No one was allowed inside the band room during this stage of the tryouts, and candidates were called up at random, so I had no idea what time Trevor competed. That hour seemed to pass by slower than a snail crossing the road, and my patience was thoroughly tested. Eventually the doors opened, and the masses exited. Most smiled and acted excited. What was the verdict?

As Trevor approached, he immediately said, "We won't know who's chosen until tonight or tomorrow." As if he read my questioning mind, he continued, saying, "The band director will be taking into consideration the ballots from the band members' top three rankings, and then he'll make his final decision. He will be calling each of us with the results when he makes his determination."

"Does that big smile on your face mean you feel like you did well?" I asked as I smiled back at my child in anticipation.

"Yea, I feel good about my performance. But then again, there were several who did a really good job. It's going to be a tight competition." At that final comment he hugged me, then headed for the car in the parking lot.

My heart skipped a beat at the sound of the phone ringing later that evening. I held my breath while Trevor answered it. I searched his face for any reaction to the news. That child should have been an actor. He had the best poker face while he listened to his band director. Finally, he said, "That's great, thank you so much." My legs nearly buckled at the realization that my child was chosen. He would be a drum major for his high school marching band, a leader of his peers. Tears of joy trickled down my cheeks, and we hugged tightly as soon as he hung up.

During the next few weeks I noticed a remarkable change in my child. He acted more mature and determined. It was as if an invisible switch had been activated, turning off his anxiety and turning on his confidence. He took his new drum major role seriously and engrossed himself in the leadership position, becoming a role model to the other students.

I recall a day when I showed up to watch the end of a practice. Another mother approached me and smiled warmly.

"I wanted to thank Trevor for being there for my daughter this past couple of weeks. She has selective mutism, too, and when Trevor shared with her that he suffers from this anxiety, she was shocked. He took her under his wing and helped her know she's not alone."

I stood there frozen by the surprise of this mother's admission. Trevor hadn't mentioned anything to me about a band member with selective mutism. How could he not have thought this was important enough to share with his own mom? I quickly pushed those negative, jealous emotions aside and focused on the positives this fellow band parent offered. My son was an amazing role model for a girl who suffered from the same anxiety. He had never met another person with selective mutism, so this was exciting. And because Trevor was so progressed with the anxiety issue, it had to be uplifting for her to meet him.

"I didn't know there was another student with selective mutism. I'm so glad Trevor could help her," I answered as I hid my disappointment over being left out of the loop.

"That's one of the things that helps my Anna feel more comfortable talking with Trevor. She knows he won't share their conversations." The other mother continued, saying, "Although, she technically hasn't used her voice with him. They just text back and forth. Unfortunately, she hasn't progressed as far as Trevor with speaking in public yet, but we're hopeful that being around him will have a positive impact on her comfort level. Just knowing there's someone else out there with selective mutism is a big deal."

Before I realized it, the practice was over, and the kids exited the building. The fellow band parent raised her hand in a quick goodbye, then proceeded toward her daughter, who was heading her way.

I stood there a moment longer, still stunned by this information. I had trouble grasping the fact that another student had selective mutism. Trevor wasn't alone. Although my logical brain already knew this to be true, meeting an actual person made it real.

Trevor was one of the last few people to leave practice. He stayed behind in case one of the other members had a question for him. I heard the laughter exchanged between him and a friend before I spotted my child. Moments like those warmed my heart. I thoroughly enjoyed it as I watched Trevor have fun with a friend. And even though those moments were common at that point in his life, I still could recall when they didn't happen at all. Within a few short years he grew out of his anxiety and into a confident person.

CHAPTER 29

Curing Selective Mutism

After the marching band season ended, there was an awards banquet. Before the festivities I decided the time was right for the band director to be made aware of Trevor's past struggles. I discussed it with Trevor first and made sure he was comfortable with the idea. Mr. Alyward, the band director, had never heard of the disorder and was astonished when he discovered one of his drum majors was diagnosed with it. He then asked if it would be ok to mention it at the awards banquet.

Mr. Alyward's speech was packed with emotion as he told Trevor's story at the banquet. He talked of a boy who silently struggled with selective mutism throughout his life and persevered through the anxiety. He continued to explain how this boy not only overcame the disorder but excelled beyond expectations as he led more than two hundred other students. The pride he felt in Trevor's accomplishments was felt by all, and the crowd joined in with cheer as Mr. Alyward revealed this boy's identity. Trevor Cox.

As Trevor stood to accept his award, I breathed deeply and held back my tearful emotion. I didn't want the tears to block my view for a single moment. This was my baby's final step from childhood to adulthood, and I was so thankful he entered it with the ability to use his voice.

Changes happened drastically within the next few years in Trevor's life. After graduation he toured Europe for a few weeks with the Ohio Ambassadors of Music program. He played his trumpet with the orchestra in concerts in various countries. Earning his spot with this band was life-altering. He had never been away from home for so long or so far. I worried about his safety and mental health while he was on tour, but he managed to check in regularly via texting and an occasional phone call. He thrived in this new life.

When Trevor was first diagnosed with selective mutism, I never would have believed such a leap was possible. My silent child had joined the world—alone. He overcame the disorder and proved he could live beyond the anxiety.

Then, the following three summers he joined a drum and bugle corps and traveled the US for competitions. Playing his instrument was a huge part of his life and allowed him the freedom to speak through music.

At this point I felt my child was finally cured. We did it—we made it to the other side of this evil anxiety. My thoughts drifted to a memory all those years ago when our psychologist said there was no cure. Pride seeped into the forefront of my mind. We must be an exception to the rule since we won the war.

The decision to write about our struggles battling selective mutism and winning had a profound impact on my life. I wanted to reach out to others and help them too. My husband encouraged me and recommended I interview our son for his side of the story. I immediately texted Trevor, who responded, "Sure. That's a good book idea." I was relieved he approved of my book plan, and he agreed to an interview.

For reasons that elude me now, I thought Trevor might have magically forgotten about having selective mutism. We focused so much energy on not bringing it to his attention throughout his life that I assumed he might not have realized he was different.

One afternoon, Trevor stopped in for lunch before his indoor percussion competition, which was happening later that evening. He stayed so busy as he balanced work, college, and band. A free moment was uncommon. I took advantage of this bit of downtime and jumped at the chance to start our interview.

"Trevor, do you remember when you were younger and suffered from selective mutism?" His sluggish mood encouraged me to continue. "I was wondering, can you recall a time when you weren't able to use your voice because of the fear of the anxiety?"

My six-foot, three-inch "child" reached out for the chair and steadied himself as he pondered my question. After a brief pause his answer spilled out of his mouth and took with it all color from his face. "Every time," he answered heavily. "I can't remember a time when I wasn't scared to talk."

His reply puzzled me, and I decided more clarification was needed to get a better answer. "Oh, I mean a specific incident that might have left a stronger memory of that fear."

Irritation grew in his voice as he responded with a question. "Why are you asking me this *now*, right before I have a competition?" His body trembled in reaction to the growing anxiousness. "You couldn't have picked a worse time to bring this up, and now I'm stressed out." He held out his shaking hand as proof of the building anxiety. "I've tried hard to push those memories down, but how can I when you're bringing it all back up?" He turned abruptly, then dashed out of the room to flee our conversation.

My mouth gaped open as I watched my child go from happy-go-lucky to instant meltdown mode. I thought he was cured. Confused by his anxious reaction, I uttered an apology to the back of his head as he left the room. I had triggered his stress and caused his anxiety to resurface. His response reminded me of someone who suffers from PTSD (post-traumatic stress disorder), but I had no desire to suggest this to him. After several minutes I chanced another apology attempt as he passed by me on his way to load his car with necessary band items for the competition. I limited my words and focused on only apologizing and not justifying. I said, "I'm sorry, I shouldn't have tried to interview you right now. I should have scheduled an interview time so you could be prepared."

Trevor's shoulders visibly relaxed as he accepted my apology. After he gave me a quick hug, he finished packing up his stuff and carried it to his car. As he pulled out of the driveway, we shared our traditional goodbye, waving the ASL "I love you" sign to one another. I said a silent prayer for the added weight I had put on my child to be lifted before he performed that evening. Then I realized we are no exception to the ugly face of selective mutism; we are the norm. There is no cure. It is a lifelong battle. But there is hope—hope for a productive, full life. While Trevor still struggles with anxiety, he has learned to overcome the fear of speaking. He has joined the world and is using his voice.

He is living beyond the silence.

Finding Hope Through Treatment

Even though my child has not won the impossible war against selective mutism, he has won many battles along the way. This realization did not deflate my motivation for reaching out to help others; the contrary held true. Knowing this is a lifelong journey with ups and downs, progress, and setbacks helped direct my focus on the true value of our life struggles. We've been there, we've faced the ugliness, and we've come out on the other side, not cured but joining in life productively. There is hope for anyone dealing with this anxiety no matter their age or severity.

If you have a child whom you suspect has selective mutism, your first step should be seeking professional help. Talk to your child's pediatrician; discuss a possible referral to a pediatric mental health specialist. Psychologists, psychiatrists, and speech-language pathologists can diagnose selective mutism. Ruling out other possible issues is a crucial step. The medical professional will diagnose your child through a series of questions and tests. The parental figures are involved in this dialogue as well as the child. However ridiculous it may sound, asking a mute child questions and receiving no verbal answers may still be quite beneficial for the doctor. They assess body language, eye contact, facial expressions, and any other response your child may or may not provide when directly questioned. This information is more important than you may realize, especially when ruling out autism, oppositional behavior, attention deficit disorder, and many other potential mental health issues. Knowing the correct diagnosis is the best way to begin your child's journey to recovery.

A speech-language pathologist (SLP aka speech therapist) often has treatment plans instrumental to overcoming selective mutism. But not every speech therapist has treated the issue, so reaching out to the right one might take a little time.

I asked more than a dozen speech therapists if they had any experience with selective mutism, and only two had ever treated the disorder. Heather L Hensley, MS CCC SLP (Masters of science with a certificate of clinical competence in speech language pathology), said the average age for which she has seen selective mutism in patients is age six. During our communication she described what a typical session may entail and offered words of wisdom on how the treatment environment can affect a child with selective mutism.

"Environmental noise and the person listening or watching plays a huge part in (the child's) communication," she said as she continued to explain the best approach in her process. "Work with teachers to encourage classroom strategies that do not single out the student while allowing for one-on-one time." Heather then discussed other treatment interventions that have brought her success, including "whispering in the classroom with the teacher and increasing volume when working one-on-one" and "behavior modification that uses a reward system for verbalizing." Another successful approach is to "use small group treatment where everyone takes turns asking questions in the students' comfortable environment." While the environment can have a huge impact on how effective the treatments are, it does not mandate success. Time and repetition are necessary, including working with the child at home under the guidance of the medical professional.

Another interaction brought more insight into this debilitating disorder. Amber Manion, MS CCC-SLP2, expanded on the environmental factor and explained her recent session with a two-and-a-half-year-old SM patient. "We started by building a positive relationship with the client and determining when they were most comfortable communicating, then developing a plan to carry that comfort to a variety of settings." She continued to explain the evaluation process. "The initial evaluation takes place in the home and is completed to assess basic development, including speech, language, and cognition. We look at how the child communicates either via pointing, sounds, words, or relying on their caregiver, and can they participate in basic activities such as a sorting shapes. It is difficult to assess selective mutism and usually requires several visits as it is more psychologically based." Amber assured me the process can work, but it does take time and continued treatments. Often the medical professional must stand back and watch the interactions of the child with those to whom they actively speak (usually a parent or sibling) and allow them time to gain trust in the therapist and comfort in speaking around them. Eventually the focus can be shifted onto the child communicating directly to the therapist, but that does not happen overnight. Time is a key factor in learning to overcome selective mutism.

Appendices

APPENDIX 1

Notes

The treatment team may extend beyond the doctor or speech therapist to include a counselor, a behavior analyst, and/or a social worker. Each offers its own direction of care. Realizing everyone involved with your child is part of the collective team will increase the success of battling selective mutism. But the biggest impact will come from you and your family. Knowledge, understanding, and patience are vital. Do your own research. Finding books on the topic is invaluable, especially books written by individuals who have selective mutism or parents of children with SM. They offer a unique perspective, having experienced it firsthand. Joining online groups geared toward selective mutism is another avenue for information and support. Chatting with other parents who are dealing with the same issue can be rewarding in knowing you are not alone. Often these groups have healthcare specialists fielding questions from around the globe. Your child is not the only person in the world suffering from selective mutism, but they are unique with their personal struggles. Posting online about your wins and fails helps strengthen your resolve in learning with your child to overcome this disorder. And reading what others have posted may give new ideas on how to approach issues. Reach out and get connected.

Whichever mental health professional or treatment approach you choose, acting quickly is important. Waiting too long without intervention can give selective mutism stronger roots, making it more difficult to overcome. The sooner you try, the quicker the recovery. The worst thing to do is nothing. Yes, I believe it's even worse than setbacks. Why? Because we can learn from what didn't work, but without trying, we have no idea how to help change happen. Theodore Roosevelt said it best. ". . . The best thing you can do is the right thing, the next best thing is the wrong thing, and the worst thing you can do is nothing." Reach out to help your child. Change starts with you in your own home with your own family. Trying to understand what your child is going through will make a positive impact on them. They will see your efforts and feel your love. This will give them security in knowing they are not alone in this fight. Don't force them to talk about what they are going through. Instead, invite them to feel comfortable discussing anything with you when they are ready. Reduce their pressure by channeling your empathy.

There is hope for recovery through this journey.

Practical Application Chapter Discussion Points

INTRODUCTION. MEETING SELECTIVE MUTISM

What is selective mutism and why is it referred to as a childhood anxiety disorder?

If you type "selective mutism" into your Google page, sources of information appear. The silent world of selective mutism unfolds, and the learning begins. Defining the disorder is an important step. Selective mutism is an anxiety that causes a person to be mute in certain situations. It is often referred to as a *childhood* anxiety disorder because typically that is when the symptoms are first noticed. But sometimes, with the right circumstances children may go years without anyone realizing there is a problem. Then, as teenagers or adults they begin to exhibit more severe symptoms, leading to a late diagnosis.

CHAPTER 1. BEATING THE BULLIES

What are unseen rules?

It is typical of someone with selective mutism to set unseen rules, which must be painstakingly followed. For example, if you have never talked to a specific person, then you cannot break those rules. You must continue to never speak to that person. This is often the perception of an untreated SM case. Hope does exist, however, and one can learn to live beyond selective mutism and other childhood anxieties. It takes time, patience, and understanding.

It is important to realize a child with anxieties does not choose to react in a certain way. Their anxiety guides their reactions, and they have not developed coping mechanisms for handling the fearful emotions that occur when faced with their triggers.

CHAPTER 2. BONDING OVER FARTING: NEW BEGINNINGS

Will my child outgrow the shyness?

Often selective mutism is overlooked or misdiagnosed. Parents may assume their child is merely shy. The first step is to get professional help as soon as possible. Even if shyness is considered to be the issue, it is not harmful to have the child evaluated by a specialist. The sooner the diagnosis is determined, the faster the recovery may be. And the opposite is also true. The longer a person exhibits bad behaviors and set patterns, the more engrained those patterns become. It takes more time and becomes more difficult to undo the learned behaviors. Early intervention is the key to quicker success.

CHAPTER 3. BEYOND SHYNESS

I'm worried my child is a little too shy. What should I do?

If you notice your child is different from other children, discuss the issue with your pediatrician. Do not wait for them to grow out of it.

Often we downplay those issues or turn a blind eye in the direction of our children. I believe it's not intentional and has nothing to do with our love for our kids. But we're too close to it; we're *in* their lives. Sometimes that makes it difficult to see the problem. If someone notices an issue with your child, don't deny the possibility. Keeping an open mind is important because having an anxiety disorder does not make your child less important than other children.

CHAPTER 4. DIAGNOSING SELECTIVE MUTISM

Is the anxiety called selective mutism because a person can select when to talk?

Selective mutism causes a person to be unable to use their voice in *select* situations. This explains the *selective* part of the name. Many believe a selectively mute child can select when or where to use their voice, but this is incorrect. The crippling fear associated with using their voice is not a conscious thought, which means they cannot control when they cannot speak. They must feel comfortable in the setting to be verbal. Often such children are only comfortable around two to three family members inside their house whom they see regularly. When anyone else tries to communicate with them, they fall mute, unable to speak.

CHAPTER 5. PROTECTIVE MOMMA BEAR

Is muteness the only symptom of selective mutism?

We've discussed the definition of selective mutism and determined it is an anxiety issue that causes muteness in certain situations. But that is only part of it. Body language is negatively impacted by SM. Lack of eye contact is a common symptom, and children with selective mutism often cower in response to the fear certain social situations evoke.

If you notice this behavior in a child, the best reaction is to reduce their stress by avoiding bringing attention to them. Don't point out that they are acting shy. Instead, redirect your focus from them.

Talking about something you see nearby may elicit a positive response in the child. They may want to also see what you are observing and may begin to raise their eyes toward this other object of interest. In time this repeated technique may help the child feel more comfortable around you, improving their body language. Little steps in the right direction should be embraced.

CHAPTER 6. FIGHTING FEAR WITH FEAR

Is it fear that prevents a person from speaking when struggling with selective mutism?

Oftentimes, those with selective mutism do not recognize their anxiety as fear, but their body responds the same way. Fear is a physical response to a perceived threat. We have this little almond-shaped part in our brains called an amygdala. (There is a pair.) The job of the amygdala is to process emotions such as fear and to cause the body to react quickly and without thought. For example, if a snake dropped from a tree and into your pathway, you would not think about making your legs move. This automatic reaction is the amygdala doing its job. It may save your life by making you react, often faster than your conscious brain is aware.

The perceived threat triggers your sympathetic nervous system, causing a fight or flight response. Everyone has it, which also means, everyone experiences fear. Our breathing quickens and heart rate increases, among other physical symptoms, when the amygdala is activated.

Each person has a different level of tolerance before the amygdala is triggered. People with selective mutism and social anxiety may have a lower threshold level inciting their fear response. And often, the fear response is toward other people. When they are in social situations, their amygdala is triggered, perceiving the people as the threat. Fear is felt. It is a physical reaction which they do not control. It is automatic. Their body responds appropriately for being placed in a threatening situation. Fight or flight occurs, or in their case, it is often freeze-mode. The fear will always be present, but the more familiar a person becomes to the symptoms that occur, the easier it is to overcome them.

CHAPTER 7. A MILESTONE: FIRST DAY OF KINDERGARTEN

Can my child get assistance at school to help with their selective mutism?

In the US public school systems, a child with a disability can get assistance. Mentioned in this chapter is an IEP (Individualized Education Program), which is a legal document for each child who has a disability and needs special education. It determines their need and a route for assistance. First, the school must decide if the child meets the criteria for an IEP. If they do not, they might still qualify for the lesser version, a 504 plan. This is a document written for a child who can still function in a regular classroom environment but might need extra time for exams or exceptions to rules due to their disorder. These plans can be instrumental in helping a child. Other countries may have similar programs. Check with your child's school to determine what type of assistance is available.

Speech therapy may be appropriate and covered under such plans. A speech-language pathologist can help the anxious child learn coping methods. They often work one-on-one with the child, in groups, or directly with the teacher. Having a school-based speech therapist may offer a unique advantage. Being in the school offers the benefit of being in the social situation causing the child to be mute. And this may aid in a faster recovery.

CHAPTER 8. THE IMPACT OF TOGETHERNESS

Should I force my child to answer me when I ask a question?

The anxiety from selective mutism can be triggered when a child feels vulnerable. In Trevor's case he was afraid to admit he was unable to use his voice in class. His fear of this disappointment from me caused him to lash out in anger. The signs were there; I simply wasn't able to read them. His first absence of speech should have alerted me that he was nervous about answering my question. It is important to give a child with selective mutism time to consider their answer. If they do not immediately share a response with you, consider offering words of encouragement. Remind them you won't be upset if they are unable to speak aloud and tell them you would appreciate knowing how their day went. This approach might get you a less angry response and more information from your child.

CHAPTER 9. GIANT LEAP OF PROGRESS

*Should I tell my child how happy I am
when they finally speak in public?*

Children with selective mutism struggle with attention directed on them, especially if it is regarding an uncomfortable topic. If you focus on their verbal accomplishments, they often feel embarrassed. The physical symptoms from this emotion become more than they can handle, and they tend to shut down. Not bringing attention to Trevor using his voice when he ordered his candy reduced the stress of the event and avoided one of his triggers. Had I said something about him talking, he might have reacted negatively, potentially preventing him from doing it again.

CHAPTER 10. USING ANGER AS AN OUTLET

How can I help my child deal with their anger issues?

Angry outbursts often become a child's coping method for processing the physical symptoms they feel when they experience uncomfortable emotions. We can provide alternative options for this anger. Deep breathing is an effective calming method. Breathe in through your nose slowly for the count of two, then out through your mouth slowly for the count of four. Repeat two to three deep breaths. This technique is especially beneficial combined with meditation.

Painting, drawing, and clay modeling are all effective artistic mediums as well as many other activities. Engaging in art often produces a calming effect and can aid in anger management. Enrolling a child in an art class or private music lessons might offer a valuable benefit and improve their angry outbursts.

CHAPTER 11. SAYING HI IN FIRST GRADE

How should I respond if my child speaks in public?

This topic has been mentioned but is worth readdressing. If a child has spoken aloud for the first time, redirecting attention elsewhere is vital. Do not bring attention to the child's successful use of verbal communication. The embarrassment of standing out could be detrimental to their progress. They may be proud of themselves for their accomplishment, but that does not mean they can handle the attention a celebration would cause. Use body language to convey excitement by offering a smile, a hug, or a kiss to your child when they speak aloud to a stranger. Do not verbally mention their accomplishment unless they do.

CHAPTER 12. SELECTIVE MUTISM IS MUCH MORE THAN BEING SILENT

Are angry outbursts a normal symptom of selective mutism?

Anger is often expressed when a child with anxieties is unable to process their emotions. It is a common outlet to rid their body of the feelings associated with selective mutism. Inadequacy, low self-esteem, loneliness, insecurity, anxiousness, embarrassment, and fear are some of the emotions involved with the disorder. When the child is faced with these overwhelming feelings, they may act out through the familiar method of anger. Kicking, screaming, throwing tantrums, and having meltdowns help the child temporarily relieve their hurtful feelings. It is important to teach them alternative methods for dealing with their inner pain. Talking to a comfort person is a big step in maturity. Using their words may seem like an impossible task when dealing with selective mutism, but once they've mastered how to express themselves verbally to someone they trust, they may be able to apply this same approach in uncomfortable situations.

Begin with teaching the child calming methods such as deep breathing, listening to music, light exercise, or visualizing themselves being calm. This is an important first step. Once the initial swell of anger is under control, they may be able to find the words to express what they are feeling. If your child is unwilling to talk to you about their fears, maybe suggest they write down their feelings or talk to a pet. If they don't have a pet, they can use an inanimate security object—for example, a stuffed animal or a photo of a loved one. Teaching them to use words to express their feelings is vital to the recovery process.

If you suspect their angry outbursts are more extreme than expected or if they occur more than three times a week, they may have disruptive mood dysregulation disorder. Trevor most likely suffered from this, but we never had him professionally diagnosed. The following are common symptoms associated with DMDD:

- Symptoms are present for at least a year.

- Severe temper outbursts occur at least three times a week.

- They are irritable, angry, or sad nearly every day.

- Their reaction is bigger than you expected.

- They are at least six years old with symptoms beginning before age ten.

If you suspect this disorder, it is advisable to seek professional help for a definitive diagnosis and treatment plan.

CHAPTER 13. BREAKTHROUGH BLESSINGS
What if my child tries to talk but fails?

Being supportive is crucial when helping a child learn to overcome selective mutism or other childhood anxieties. Our parental love should be unconditional. Make it clear to your child that your love is unfaltering and does not hinge on their verbal skills. Sometimes their fear of disappointing you may hinder their progress and they believe if they don't try, they can't fail. Encourage your child but remind them you will be proud no matter the outcome. If they realize failing is part of the learning process, they may have more courage to try to use their voice. Talk to your child, and they may surprise you.

CHAPTER 14. A SHRED OF NORMALCY
Is my child being rude intentionally?

Children with selective mutism typically are too afraid to show emotion. Others often misinterpret their lack of response as rudeness. The anxiety is too overwhelming for the child to acknowledge their appreciation.

Making others aware that your child has difficulty displaying emotion may help to prevent them from drawing their own conclusions about your SM child. Don't expect your child to say "thank you" or "please," but do allow them the opportunity. If they say nothing after an acceptable amount of time, then it is ok to offer those words for them. But always give them a chance. They may surprise you one day.

CHAPTER 15. LEFT OUT
Why does my SM child hate having their picture taken?

Body language is a form of communication. In a child suffering from selective mutism, body language is negatively impacted. They are not comfortable displaying emotion.

Although (as previously mentioned) lack of eye contact is a common issue with the disorder, it is not the only symptom. Often SM children do not want to be in pictures, especially when others are involved. This social behavior causes anxiousness, and they may refuse to be included. When they do participate, they either grimace or give only a hint of a smile. School photos often capture a misinterpreted expression of anger from their scowls. But it is not anger they are portraying—it is fear. Help your child prepare for school photo day. Explain to them how each child will have their photo taken, that no one is omitted. Maybe show them your old school photos to help prepare them. But if they come home with angry faces in their pictures, try to understand and not take it personally. They are not trying to upset you; they were the ones upset. Don't expect them to smile but be happy if they do.

CHAPTER 16. BABYSITTER BLUES

Is separation anxiety a symptom of selective mutism?

It is common for a child with selective mutism to exhibit co-disorders. The extreme stubbornness Trevor displayed when standing at the babysitter's front door for four hours is not typical of SM, but it can be explained by separation anxiety. This problem affects approximately four to five percent of US children in ages ranging from seven to eleven, being less common in teenagers and adults. The child with separation anxiety is fearful of being alone and may refuse to leave the home or be separated from a loved one. Most cases do not need clinical intervention, but if the symptoms persist too long, professional help is advisable. In some cases separation anxiety may be a reflection of the parent's fears. Their child senses this apprehension and responds accordingly.

Reducing your child's anxiety is the first approach to overcoming separation anxiety. But keep your own anxieties in check. How are you responding to a new environment? Is your child sensing your fears and internalizing them? This brings us back to the importance of communication with your child. Explain to them the reasons for requiring the new situations. Make sure they understand the separation will not last forever. Positive reinforcement may aid in overcoming this anxiety issue. Offering a small token such as a toy or a certain snack to enjoy after being reunited may give them the motivation to succeed in the new situation.

CHAPTER 17. SECOND GRADE INTRODUCTIONS

If my child unintentionally talks, is it ok to tell them I heard them?

This may sound redundant, but it is worthy of repetition. If a child slips and speaks aloud, you mustn't bring attention to the success. They may not have intended to talk. And if you acknowledge hearing their voice, they may not do it again. Ignoring them when the accidental speaking occurs may offer reassurance. They may develop control over their fear and attempt to use their voice again intentionally.

Offer your child opportunities to speak, but do not force them. Visiting playgrounds with other children present may encourage your child to talk.

CHAPTER 18. TREVOR TALKS!

Will my child remain mute forever?

Often we worry our children who struggle with selective mutism will remain mute forever. It seems like an impossible turnaround for them to be able to overcome the fear imposed by the disorder and use their voice on command. But there is hope. Patience during therapy does pay off. Without forcing your child, they will blossom into the person they are intended to be. Your job is to offer encouragement along the way. Be there physically and emotionally for your child. But remember to hold back from acknowledging their failures or accomplishments. Any unsolicited attention toward them may cause setbacks in their journey to speak aloud. Even if they bring it to your attention, tread carefully with your words. Too much emphasis may still increase their anxiety. Try to avoid using words such as *talk, speak, say*, or any other phrasing that brings attention to them using their voice. Instead, listen to them, and then respond with, "That's great," "Wonderful," "Glad to hear," or any other positive reinforcement.

CHAPTER 19. OVERCOMING SELECTIVE MUTISM

How can I get my child to talk to extended family members?

Invisible rules are frequently set and followed by those suffering from selective mutism. These set patterns are familiar and comfortable. The child is unsure of what may happen if they speak or make eye contact with someone, so they avoid these actions. Fear of the unknown holds them back.

Helping your child break these rules and develop new patterns is important to the recovery process. Instead of expecting your child to talk to an extended family member in their home, bring that family member into your home or another comfortable setting. If you reduce the stresses, your child may be more successful. Patience and repetition are necessary. Even with the familiar environment, the child may not be able to speak to the family member initially. But in time their comfort may increase, and new patterns may develop. They may begin to talk to that person as their learned comfort increases. It is important to approach one change at a time before adding another. So, don't try to add two or three new people into the mix. The child most likely will only be able to handle one new person or change in their life at a time.

CHAPTER 20. SCHOOL PRESENTATIONS READ ALOUD

Is it helpful to teach a SM child specific phrases appropriate for certain questions even if they are not speaking to others yet?

It is important to help prepare a child with selective mutism for other childhood anxieties that tax their courage. Be clear with them and explain what they can expect when presented with a fearful task. Knowing what to expect and what is expected of them may make the difference between their success or failure. Understanding what the task involves and what they need to do may reduce their anxiety. Role-playing may help them act out the assignment. They need to understand the variables. Give the child examples of how they can react appropriately to their duties. Children who are aware of what to say often speak sooner than those who do not. It is easier to recall a memorized sentence than it is to pull words from a terrified brain. Practice, practice, practice.

CHAPTER 21. LEO THE LION FINDS HIS VOICE
How can I reduce my child's stress with talking?

It is important to inform the SM child of information regarding them. But limit the stress you place on them by avoiding engagement in the decision-making process. The adults should be making the decisions, but the child deserves to know what's going on. Keep them in the loop.

Facing fear is a perfect opportunity for the recovery process. In our situation Trevor faced the fear of speaking to his preschool teacher. If it had been a candid chat, I am convinced he would have remained mute in that moment. But he had a script and knew exactly what to say. He didn't have to think about the words; he simply read them. Try this technique with your child. Write out a note they can read to another. The words on the paper may make the task easier. If it doesn't work the first time, however, try not to express your disappointment. Instead, focus on patience. Sometimes this trick takes multiple attempts before it is successful. Also, having the child write the note increases the success rate. If it is written in their words, they are more likely to read it aloud.

CHAPTER 22. QUIET GESTURES MAKE LOUD IMPRESSIONS
Should I keep my child busy with daily extracurricular activites?

We want to offer our children the best childhood possible, filled with fun experiences, but overloading your child's schedule may do more harm than good with their anxiety. Look for ways to reduce the chaos. Don't go out every night of the week to add stimulation. Instead, focus on a couple of days of fun and allow your child time to decompress the other times. This may aid in a speedy recovery.

And remember, selective mutism is only one element of your child. It is not their entire identity. They have dreams, desires, and goals in life that do not include the anxiety disorder. Help them achieve their life's ambitions by supporting them and offering your love. There is an amazing child hidden under all that anxiety.

CHAPTER 23. GAINING A FURRY FRIEND

Is it better to isolate my child to help lessen their social stress?

Your child should be given opportunities to make friends with other children. This is necessary for learning to overcome selective mutism. If they stay isolated, they may never learn how to handle the fear associated with being around other people. The scouts, 4H club, team sports, and playgroups may be good options for children to socialize. Look for local groups that engage children. Often the local library will sponsor youth classes and offer storytime.

Your involvement is valuable for the child's comfort during a new social activity. Plus, it allows you to gauge if the activity is too stressful for your child to handle. Structured groups often reduce stress for children since they know what to expect, and so they can follow their set behaviors. The earlier you introduce other children into your child's life, the better. If your child is around other children often, they may learn coping skills at an earlier age, so they may learn to speak to others quicker.

CHAPTER 24. RUNNING FOR STUDENT COUNCIL

What is the best way to approach large projects or tasks?

If your child has been assigned a big task, being prepared is important. Like all stressors for selective mutism, tackling large tasks requires understanding. First, open communication with your child regarding the assignment. Find out the details and expectations involved. Talk with your child about these expectations so they are fully aware of their role. Then, approach the assignment in sections to help prevent them from feeling overwhelmed. Often people quit trying when the obstacle they face appears too large a hurdle. So, reducing it into smaller sections makes it less threatening and easier to tackle. This applies to most anxiety-related mindsets but is more challenging for younger children with selective mutism. One cannot succeed unless they first try.

CHAPTER 25. BENEFITS OF ANIMAL THERAPY

Would a pet be good or bad for my child's anxiety?

Pets are a wonderful addition to any family, but for a child with anxieties, they can be life-changing. Any pet can be used as an emotional support animal to offer companionship. The pet does not need any special training for this type of assistance. If you decide to take on a pet, it is important to allow your child to choose what kind of animal they would prefer, and you must be ready to help take care of that pet. Don't expect your child will do everything necessary for their care (scooping litter boxes, taking a dog out to potty, bathing, feeding, taking them to the vet, etc.). It is beneficial to include your child in the care of the pet, but don't place too much stress on them. The whole point of an emotional support animal is to provide your child with companionship without increasing their anxiety by adding responsibilities.

If you are unable to take on the responsibility of a permanent pet, consider other options for pet exposure. Visit friends who have pets, volunteer with your child at a local pet adoption center, enroll your child in a horse camp (as we did with Trevor), or consider pet sitting a couple of days each week in your home. (There are pet apps for this—check out *Rover* or *Wag* for good examples.)

A service animal is trained for a specific task to help disabled people. They are often used with those who have physical disabilities and are wheelchair-bound, but they can be helpful for those with mental disabilities too. They are quite expensive due to their extensive training. I feel an emotional support pet offers enough value, especially for the price (often free, depending on the animal), but it does depend on the mental health level of your child. Speak to your child's doctor about this option for further exploration.

CHAPTER 26. TREVOR'S VETERANS DAY SPEECH

Will my child ever be able to talk in public?

Sometimes it is difficult to remain optimistic, especially when we see our children struggle. We often get as discouraged as they do. When Trevor was mute, I never would have believed he would someday be a public speaker. In only a few short years his life changed drastically. There is hope for all the silent children struggling to find their voice. Patience and encouragement can help them learn to overcome the fears selective mutism creates. Don't give up on someone with SM. Have faith.

CHAPTER 27. SAYING GOODBYE TO GRANDMA

Will changing schools cause my child to regress with their SM?

Change of environment may have a positive impact on a child struggling with the anxiety of selective mutism. Granted, too much change may overstimulate them. But offering change at the right time in their progression may improve their confidence, especially if their old habits are preventing them from speaking aloud.

If your child is still unable to use their voice, there is great hope when entering a new school. Initially they may express worry about starting at a new school, but in time they may realize the benefit, especially with your guidance. This big change allows the child an opportunity to forge a new path. It may boost their confidence and encourage them to speak aloud when surrounded by unfamiliar students.

CHAPTER 28. FROM STRUGGLER TO LEADER

No one in my city has heard of SM, we feel alone. What can we do?

Often a child with selective mutism or other childhood anxieties believes they are alone in their struggles. Until they meet someone else with a similar issue, it is hard for them to accept that there are others. Enrolling your child in a group counseling session with other children who have similar issues may help provide support and reduce their feelings of isolation. Selective mutism is uncommon, so it may be difficult to find a local group. But there are online options for group meetings.

CHAPTER 29. CURING SELECTIVE MUTISM

Is there a cure for selective mutism?

Anxiety does not permanently disappear, which means selective mutism does not completely go away. Understanding this helps us to accept the lifelong setbacks that can occur with the disorder. However, once your child has found the ability to deal with the fear of using their voice outside of their comfort zone, they will be living beyond their own silence. They will have learned to overcome the biggest struggle of selective mutism.

Continue to help prepare your child when they are faced with obstacles in life. Having a plan and knowing what to expect is always the best approach. Had I scheduled a time to interview Trevor, his anxiety episode might have been prevented. Expecting him to handle the stress easily when he was distracted was the wrong approach. As parents we may do the wrong thing with the right intentions. All we can do is our best. If your first approach doesn't work, try a different way, but keep trying. Your child deserves the effort.

APPENDIX 3

Treatment Options

Children with selective mutism are believed to learn set patterns for coping with the anxiety. Behavioral strategies target these patterns and focus on helping the child learn new ways of dealing with the fear. Not all the treatment options will fit your specific needs—maybe only one or two will be appropriate for your child. These ideas are not intended to replace the expertise of a medical professional. They are offered to help you understand the treatments often used in the clinical setting.

Here are a few references for professional assistance:

Child Mind Institute, 101 E 56th St, New York, NY 10022 | (212) 308-3118 | childmind.org

Smart Center, 505 N. Old York Road, Jenkintown Sq, Lower Level, Jenkintown, PA 19046 | (215) 887-5748 | selectivemutismcenter.org.

Dr. Angela McHolm, 490 York Rd, Bldg A, Suite 211, Guelph, Ontario, Canada N1E 3J1 | (519) 830-6712 | Email: Dr_McHolm@AngelaMcHolm.com

These are two of the most popularly sought treatment centers in the eastern US and a clinic in Canada, but they are not the only options. Research your area for selective mutism treatment facilities. Ask for references and interview them before you decide which place is best for your specific needs. Your comfort with a center will impact your receptiveness to their treatment approaches.

Upon researching treatment options, I found a plethora of information from the American Speech-Language-Hearing Association's (ASHA) website: asha.org. Below I've summarized a few of the key items you may find valuable. An experienced speech therapist would be aware of these treatment options and may offer more insight into their individual success rates.

Stimulus Fading

The SM child speaks with their comfort person (the person with whom they normally verbalize) while an unfamiliar person enters the room. This person will stay quiet and watch for a few sessions, then work up to conversing with the comfort person and eventually speaking to the SM child. After the SM child develops the courage to verbalize to the unfamiliar person, a second unfamiliar person is brought in, and the process is repeated.

Shaping Technique

This technique focuses on using positive incentives as rewards. The SM child is encouraged to mouth or whisper words. The small rewards continue until the gestures increase into speaking words.

Desensitization

Relaxation techniques (deep breathing, calming music, light exercise, and/or redirecting their focus by imagining they are in a safe place) are used to help control the SM child's physical responses to fear while gradually increasing the anxiety-provoking stimuli. This teaches the child how to handle their physical reactions when faced with fear.

Exposure-Based Practice

The SM child is instructed to say certain words while slowly increasing their anxiety-provoking stimuli.

Nonverbal Communication

To encourage interactions with others, the therapist will have the SM child use pictures, drawings, writing, symbols, objects, and/or gestures for communication. Careful monitoring is necessary to ensure the child does not use this method to replace verbal communication. It is intended to increase their comfort when engaging with others, working up to using their voice.

Self-Modeling

This involves recording the SM child talking while in a comfortable environment. Then, the video or audio is replayed when the child is in an uncomfortable setting, typically around others with whom they do not speak (in homes of extended family members, church, school, or similar settings). Initially the child will hear the recording while away from the group but still in view of them. The goal of this technique is to increase the child's confidence and prepare them for speaking in other settings.

Acknowledgments

To my husband, Nick. You believed in me even before I did, and your faith never wavered.

To my son, Trevor. Your creativity shines through your art. With your cover design you portrayed the emotion of your youthful self while struggling with selective mutism. You are the life of this story.

To my son, Josh. You were there for all my technical questions and were willing to drop your own life to help mine.

To my cousin, Brian. You held me accountable every week and inspired me to give my all.

To my sister, Sharon, for lending an ear and listening to my countless rambles about this book.

Trevor's art - elementary school

About the Author

Gaye James has lived through the struggles of selective mutism by raising a child with the voice-paralyzing anxiety. Helping her son along his path of overcoming selective mutism has inspired her to reach out and advocate for others suffering with the same disorder.

Gaye spent the first half of her career helping people learn to walk through physical therapy, working as a licensed physical therapist assistant. Now, she is using the power of words to help others learn to overcome their internal fear and communicate.

Gaye lives in Dayton, Ohio with her husband and enjoys hiking, spending time with her friends, photography, and geocaching. Her two adult sons live nearby. At present, the only grandchildren are two adorable furry four-legged felines named Woodford and Hamilton.

About the Artist

Trevor Cox is the life force behind this book. He created the cover art conveying the emotion of his silent journey through the darkness of selective mutism with shining hope within reach. Scattered artwork throughout the book is also attributed to Trevor's creativity.

He is intelligent, imaginative, has a great sense of humor, and an even greater work ethic.

Throughout his struggles with selective mutism, Trevor used art as an outlet for the anxiety, allowing a productive emotional expression.

Now an adult, Trevor still has an eye for art and a passion for the digital platform. He freelances in project design and is working his way through college towards a graphic art design degree. Trevor lives in Dayton, Ohio and enjoys spending time with his cat, Hamilton, named after the ten dollar bill paid for his adoption and the Broadway show.

You may contact Trevor for project estimates via LinkedIn: Trevor Cox

About the Publisher

AuthorAcademyElite.com

Your Next Steps
in the Journey Through
Selective Mutism

✓ Visit gayejames.com for more information on selective mutism.

✓ Sign up on the website to be a member of the Silent Tribe and receive updates from the author.

✓ Inform your friends and family about the world of selective mutism. Spread your knowledge to help others understand this debilitating disorder.

✓ Be on the lookout for Gaye's next book, featuring her son, Trevor, as an illustrator—a new children's book geared toward preschoolers–second graders to help them through their struggles with selective mutism. Every child needs to know they are not alone.

✓ Visit social media sites and share Gaye's inspiration, helping spread awareness of selective mutism:

- Instagram – gayejames33
- Twitter – gayejames33
- Facebook group – Selective Mutism - Living Beyond the Silence
- LinkedIn: Gaye James

CPSIA information can be obtained
at www.ICGtesting.com
Printed in the USA
BVHW041339161120
593260BV00012B/82